DAWN OF THE PROMISED LAND

DAWN OF THE PROMISED LAND

Ben Wicks

BLOOMSBURY

First published in Great Britain 1997
Bloomsbury Publishing PLC, 38 Soho Square
London W1V 5DF

Copyright © 1997 by Ben Wicks
The moral right of the author has been asserted

Photographs Courtesy of the State of Israel
Government Press Office

A CIP catalogue record for this book
is available from the British Library

ISBN 0 7475 3292 3

10 9 8 7 6 5 4 3 2 1

Typeset by Hewer Text Composition Services, Edinburgh
Printed in Great Britain by Clays Ltd, St Ives plc

For
Monty and Blema Mazin

Foreword
by
The Honourable Shimon Peres
(Winner of the Nobel Peace Prize)

In charting the founding of any country, it may be said that "history is to a nation what memory is to the individual". But what is to be said about the singular nature of Israel's birth, whose national history reflects the collective memories and experience of all those individuals who served as its midwives – who in a real sense participated in its birth? How does the historian capture the essence of such an event, its significance to a people and to the world community?

Erich Fromm offers an important clue in his recognition that "Man himself is the most important creation and achievement of the continuous human effort – the record of which we call history". Tracing the struggle of those who were intimately involved in the creation of Israel, those who cleared the fields as well as those who cleared the political hurdles, can indeed give life to our bitter-sweet history as a nation.

In many respects, the story of any one individual recounted in this chronicle is the story of us all; hope contending with despair, accomplishment tempered by failure, triumph forever coloured by personal and national tragedy. This is our legacy. T. S. Eliot remarked that the historical sense involves a perception not only of the "pastness of the past", but of its "presence in the present".

One cannot understand Israel at fifty without understanding

the tumultuous collective memory of those who gathered expectantly, even fearfully, on Rothschild Boulevard in Tel Aviv half a century ago. The simple beauty of this effort by internationally acclaimed author Ben Wicks is in his recognition that no record of the rebirth of a sovereign Jewish state can be as compelling as the vivid recollections of those who witnessed – nay, participated in – its birth.

With echoes of the Holocaust and European persecution still ringing in their ears, these courageous pioneers chose hope over despair. Undaunted by a hostile landscape born of centuries of neglect, these determined adventurers chose to reclaim a land and turn failure into great accomplishment. And, most importantly, with peace so tantalisingly close, these "lovers of Zion" will not yield to the tragedies of the past fifty years and will yet see the triumphant reign of peace.

"Pray for the peace of Jerusalem, all who love her." Such was the call of King David 3,000 years ago. That remains the final chapter today, for Jews, Christians and Muslims alike.

Acknowledgements

It is now almost fifty years since a group of people assembled in a small museum and signed a document which would confirm the birth of a new nation. However, few countries in the world have ever suffered the kind of pain that brought Israel to that memorable point.

For me, there was only one way to tell Israel's remarkable story, and that was to draw on the experiences of those who had lived through all the peaks and troughs, all the joy and tears which finally made the signing of the Proclamation of Independence possible.

I made many new friends on my visit to Israel to prepare the material for this project. Their enthusiasm for my work left me grateful but exhausted, and they both helped me make contact with the remarkable people whose stories you will find in this book and facilitated the telling of those stories.

Because I am a great believer in fate, it does not surprise me that, on my arrival in Jerusalem, I met Wendy Elliman (Orbaum), who wrote a story about my visit for the *Jerusalem Post*. Wendy subsequently turned out to be one of the best researchers I have ever had, and, more importantly, a valued new friend. Many of the interviews in Israel were conducted by Wendy, who, with her husband Sam and their triplets to care for, showed me that she is, in addition to being a first-class journalist, also a brilliant juggler!

Robert Ritter, National Executive Director of the Canada–Israel Committee, introduced me to many friends in Israel, and constantly inspired me through his obvious pride in what the country had achieved. I am most grateful to Rob and his colleagues at the CIC for their support and encouragement. The Ministry of Foreign Affairs in Jerusalem – and in particular the Israeli Ambassador to Canada, His Excellency David Suttan – leapt forward to offer their help, and so enabled me to contact locally government officials who were equally generous with their help and advice.

My remarkable assistant Joanne Dicaire once again waded through page after page of my text, making invaluable comments. My agent and friend of twenty-five years is Matie Molinaro; and my comrade Monty Mazin is also my interviewer and researcher in Canada. Francesca (Hassida) David wielded my tape-recorder and not only conducted interviews herself, but was always on hand when I needed any translation from Hebrew into English. My friend Penny Phillips in London had the magic touch of being able to take my raw manuscript and transform it into a book ready for publication.

My wife of forty-one years, Doreen, was once again there for me at every sigh and at every turn, to encourage me and to remind me of all the important dates in the lives of our three children and eight grandchildren!

Introduction

I started out with the intention of telling the story of the birth of the modern state of Israel, but the book I wrote turned out to be more than that. This is the story of a people which through its incredible courage overcame obstacles that most of us would find insurmountable. In doing so, it carved out a home.

The Jews who chose to leave the lands of their birth to go and forge a homeland in Palestine were not faced with an easy decision. They often had to leave friends and loved ones behind. "My father was a strong man," remembers one, "and able to bear pain; but that morning he just stood there, tears rolling down his cheeks." Some had to abandon considerable wealth, luxury and status, exchanging mansions in European cities for tents in sun-baked deserts as they joined the Aliyah, the journey to the Promised Land from around the world. "I cheerfully sold all our furniture, our curtains, the iron, even the fur collar from my old winter coat," remembers another. Many have never shaken off a nostalgia for forests, green fields, the grey cities of Europe and the sight and sensation of rain. The succeeding generations, those born in Israel, have no memories to spark such yearnings.

Those who made the Aliyah in the time of the British Mandate, under which Palestine had been governed by Britain since the First World War, came by ship and train; by bus, in lorries and on foot: hundreds of thousands of Jews determined to make a new life for themselves and their families on a strip of land which hugged the eastern shore of the Mediterranean. Into this landscape came European intellectuals and idealistic thinkers, shoulder to shoulder with peasants from the *shtetls* who had yet to learn to read and write. Many could not speak Hebrew, but they clung to the radical belief that only by working for themselves could the Jews liberate themselves from the mentality of the ghetto, and this belief fuelled their determination to make the desert land bloom; each also believed profoundly in the right of the Jews to reclaim their ancestral homeland. There were those who were shocked to find that their dream would begin in a tent pitched on some barren hillside, but they quickly adapted – they had to; and whatever their background, city intellectual or village labourer, Sephardic shepherd or Ashkenazy schoolteacher, they all came with hope and idealism, and with dreams of peace, freedom, security and solidarity.

Their success in taming a land that had lain untended and malaria-ridden for centuries is a story of human triumph over adversity which few other nations can equal.

Who were these remarkable people? Most of them were members of persecuted families from all over the world. In the closing years of the last century and the opening years of this one, they journeyed from a turbulent Russia – escaping first from pogroms, later from the ferment of the communist revolution, fleeing the Red and White Guards who terrorised the streets, and taking with them only what they could carry. Later, those who could escaped from Nazi Germany and the countries that fell under Hitler's sway. Britain incurred worldwide disapproval for its policy of turning back shiploads of illegal Jewish immigrants, especially between 1939 and 1947, but 60,000 people managed to run the blockade, and by the end of the Second World War there were 600,000 Jews in Palestine: many had lost their entire families in the death camps of Germany and Eastern Europe; almost all had lost at least one relative.

What do these people who built a nation out of rock and sand have in common? Each one can look back with pride to a period of pain, courage and endurance. The people whose stories you are about to read were incredibly generous with their time. I asked each of them to relive his or her past and they willingly shared with me their memories of devotion and love, of hardship, disappointment and triumph.

The tales they told me make up a story of courage in the midst of deprivation, and of new life springing from the wilderness. It is the story of the birth of a nation – a home for the Jewish people, who had been wanderers for so long: a home called Israel.

Chapter One: Birth

The sound of the crowd gathering outside filtered into the hall. The people who had spent the last few hours on step-ladders, hanging flags and bunting on the walls and from the ceiling, felt happy and expectant. Although they'd only had a bare $200 to spend on decorations, what was there lent a great sense of importance to the occasion. The Tel Aviv Museum was not an imposing place; yet on this day, 14 May 1948, those present knew that the little building was about to become a site of central historical importance. Later that day the Proclamation of Independence of the new State of Israel would be signed there.

The museum on Rothschild Boulevard had originally belonged to Tel Aviv's first mayor, who had given it to the city for use as an art gallery. That day, the few paintings of nudes which hung on the walls had been covered, for fear that they would detract from the gravity of the occasion. The windows had been blacked out, in case of air-raids.

The cleaning staff had finished their work and were stretching and easing their aching backs. The hours of scrubbing and polishing they had put in were about to be rewarded, for they were to be among the few fortunate enough to witness the signing of the document which would herald the birth of the new nation. In later years, they would recollect the moment for their children and their grandchildren. Outside, the people who had been thronging the pavement for hours managed only to catch a glimpse of the arriving dignitaries for whom seats inside the museum had been reserved. Only 200 had been invited, all of them prominent men and women well known to the onlookers.

The lead-up to 14 May had not been easy, and many of the faces of those arriving to witness the ceremony showed signs of strain. It had been difficult for the People's Administration and the People's Council to decide whether to declare independence on the day the British Mandate ended or to postpone the proclamation until a later date. They had opted for postponement, but it had been a risk. Even those governments friendly to the tiny Yishuv – the Jewish community in Palestine – feared that the Jews would find it impossible to withstand the armies of the hostile Arab countries which surrounded them.

The US Secretary-of-State, George Marshall, had advised the Zionist leadership against proclaiming the State of Israel, warning them that they risked annihilation. (Zionism, the movement for the establishment of a Jewish state, had been founded by the journalist Theodor Herzl as long ago as 1897. Herzl had covered the Dreyfus trial for a Viennese paper in 1894, and the anti-Semitism it aroused had affected him deeply.) Despite their awareness of the danger, the People's Administration believed that the Jewish people had waited long enough and, by a majority vote taken on 12 May 1948, they decided that the time had come for Jews everywhere to have a home of their own. In part this decision was based on recent experience of the Nazi regime. There had to be somewhere in the world where Jews could go and be guaranteed a refuge from persecution. Virtually no country had offered unconditional help to the Jews of Europe during the war.

Marshall's warning was well founded. Immediately after the Proclamation, Jordan, Egypt, Iraq, Syria and Lebanon declared war. The periods of peace in the decades that followed would always be uneasy, though the ferocity and the efficiency of the Israel Defence Forces won the nation respect and ensured that annihilation, although it remained a threat, never became a reality.

But dealing with belligerent neighbours was only one problem among many for the nascent state. There were more challenges to be addressed. The day of the Proclamation came too soon for some of even the most basic wrinkles to have been ironed out. An early-morning meeting to decide on the name of the state and the final formulation of the Proclamation had hit a snag. This concerned the question, arising from an argument which took place on 13 May, about whether or not to include a reference to God in the wording of the Proclamation of Independence. The matter was finally resolved when it was agreed that the last sentence of the speech should read: "With trust in the Rock of Israel, we set our hand to this Declaration, at this Session of the Provisional State Council, on the soil of the Homeland, in the city of Tel Aviv, on this Sabbath eve, the fifth of Iyar, 5708, the fourteenth of May, 1948." David Ben-Gurion, the sixty-two-year-old socialist provisional Prime Minister, who in his lifelong devotion to the cause of Jewish nationalism had always combined his visionary talent with great pragmatism, hoped that the phrase "Rock of Israel" was sufficiently nebulous to satisfy those Jews opposed to any document which sought to establish a Jewish state containing a specific reference to God.

The final agreement had not been reached easily. Rabbi Fishman-Maimon, spokesman for the Jewish religious political parties, declared that he would agree to "Rock of Israel" only if the words "and its Redeemer" were added. To complicate the issue further, Aaron Zisling, of the left wing of the Labour Party, declared forcefully that he would never sign a document which referred in any way to a God in whom he did not believe. And the state they were founding would be a secular one.

It took Ben-Gurion most of the morning of 14 May to persuade the various parties involved to agree to his compromise solution. He explained that the meaning of the "Rock of Israel" was really twofold: while to many Jews it signified God, it could also be seen to signify the strength of the Jewish people. In the end, Rabbi Maimon agreed that the word "Redeemer" could be left out of the text.

Ironically, the first English-language translation of the text, released that day for distribution abroad, made no reference to the "Rock of Israel". The Military Censor had decided that, since the Proclamation mentioned the time and the place of the ceremony, he would remove the entire last sentence (which is also the last paragraph) as a security measure.

In his book *Ben-Gurion, Prophet of Fire* Dan Kurzman

recounts how once the copy for the Proclamation had been typed it was handed to a secretary, Dorit Rosen, who secured it in a cardboard binder to protect it until the document could be transferred to parchment. It still remained for the document to be taken from the Zionist meeting to the museum.

Zeev Sharef felt honoured to have been chosen for this task. As he watched the Zionist leaders hurry away from the meeting place, Kayemet Hall, he went to the taxi stand, intending to follow the group. Unfortunately, the last of the cabs had been taken, and to his horror he found himself stranded without any means of transport to take him to the museum. He grabbed a nearby policeman and, waving their arms desperately, they stopped the first car and asked the driver for a lift.

'Sorry,' the man replied, 'but I'm rushing home to hear the Declaration of Independence on the radio.'

Sharef, now frantic, screamed in the man's ear, 'If you don't take us to the museum you may *never* hear the Declaration of Independence, because it's right here!'

The 200 people invited to take part in the ceremony made their way from their cars and up the entrance steps into the museum, where they walked down a narrow corridor to the room where the signing was to take place. It was filled with rows of chairs facing a long table behind which thirteen members of the Provisional Government took their places beneath a large portrait of Theodor Herzl.

At exactly 4 p.m., David Ben-Gurion stood up and rapped a gavel. Then he glanced up to a gallery where, at his signal, an orchestra was supposed to start playing the *Hatikvah* (The Hope), the chosen anthem of the new nation. But no sound came. In the haste of the preparations there had been a mix-up and no orchestra had arrived. It was no matter. The assembled company rose as one, and, with tears in their eyes, began to sing the national anthem *a cappella*.

When the last notes of the anthem had faded away and the assembly had once more taken their seats, Ben-Gurion cleared his throat and announced, "I will now read the Scroll of Independence."

It took a mere fifteen minutes to declare that the State of Israel, *Eretz Yisroël*, heir to ancient Judea, Hebron and Samaria, had been born.

Chapter Two: Promised Land

For thousands of years, Palestine remained barren and ignored by those in search of wealth and power; yet this narrow strip of coastal land could claim to be home to three of the greatest religions in the world, Christianity, Islam and Judaism – a fact which caused many to think of the country as the Promised Land.

After the death of Solomon towards the end of the tenth century BC the historical kingdom of the Jews was divided in two: Israel to the north and Judea to the south. Israel lasted for about 200 years before being overrun by the Assyrians, who scattered the tribes; Judea fell to Nebuchadnezzar of Babylon in 587 BC. From then on the coastal strip was ruled first by the Macedonians, then the Egyptians, then the Romans. Under Constantine the Great the Roman Empire adopted Christianity as its official religion, and by the middle of the fifth century AD many of the people of Palestine had converted to the new faith. The Jews were allowed into Jerusalem only once a year, on the anniversary of the destruction of the temple by Nebuchadnezzar.

Then, in 614, Palestine was overrun by the Persians, who were succeeded in 632 – only two years after the death of Mohammed – by the Arabs. These rulers were liberal, but 400 years later they were replaced by the Seljuks, whose brutality towards the

Christians triggered the Crusades, which went on intermittently for 200 years, until the last Christian stronghold, at Acre, fell to the Turks in 1291. Thereafter, Palestine was under one form or another of rule by neighbouring Muslim states until 1517, when it became an annex of the Turkish Ottoman Empire. So it remained, all but forgotten, for exactly 400 years.

In 1914, an assassination in Sarajevo resulted in guns thundering throughout Europe. Turkey threw in its lot with Kaiser Wilhelm II, and Palestine, which up until then had sat quietly in the backwaters of the world, suddenly found itself to be of great strategic importance. The British, concerned about access to the Indian subcontinent via the Suez Canal, and with an emotional and religious attachment to Jerusalem which dated back to the Crusades, saw the area as vital to their interests in the Middle East. Palestine was part of the crumbling Ottoman Empire. It was enemy territory and had to be taken.

By 1917, Britain and Germany were locked in a kind of grim stalemate. Stuck in the mud of the Western Front, thousands of young men were dying every day in the filth of the trenches that snaked their way across hundreds of miles of French soil. At such a time, Britain needed all the help it could get.

The idea of an autonomous Jewish Brigade was originally proposed by Vladimir Ze'ev Jabotinsky. It found a champion in Chaim Weizmann, an eminent expatriate Polish chemist and Zionist leader living in London. Weizmann had opposed the idea initially, but once he had understood its long-term benefits, he worked for it unstintingly. Within a relatively short time, the Zion Mule Corps was established as an all-Jewish ammunition supply group, and it served with distinction on the Middle-East/Palestine front. Weizmann lived to see the foundation of the State of Israel in 1948 and became its first President.

Meanwhile, events in Russia had taken a dramatic turn. The Russian Army began to collapse as soldiers deserted in their hundreds of thousands. The Tsar was deposed in April 1917, and days later Lenin was travelling from Zurich to Petrograd via Germany – the Germans helping him in exchange for a promise of a cessation of hostilities. In the months of the Russian Revolution which followed, many Jews, who had already endured years of official discrimination and bloody pogroms, decided that the time had come to leave.

The father of D was a wealthy Jew living in Odessa. He arrived home one day and made an astonishing announcement, as D remembers:

'Pack up everything you can; we're leaving,' he said. It was not easy. We were living a very comfortable life, with servants and everything. Nevertheless my mother, father, two brothers and I left with just as much as we could carry, and we set off for Palestine. We had months of travel ahead of us. First there was a ship to Sevastopol, then another across the Black Sea to Istanbul. After that we travelled down to the Lebanon, and finally we arrived in Beirut. In Beirut we got hold of a horse and cart, and with our belongings aboard we set off for Haifa. The first impression was awful. The city was full of beggars and paupers. And there were blind people everywhere, too – most of them suffering from glaucoma.

Fortunately for us, we had made friends with a fellow traveller who advised us to make for a place called Petach-Tikvah, near Tel Aviv. We followed his advice and settled there among the orange groves and the almond groves, where Father was able to get work shelling almonds. Eventually, he opened a small store, but he hated it. In the meantime, though, he was studying English and eventually he passed an exam which enabled him to become a schoolteacher.

Then, as my father had a profession, we were able to return to Haifa, where we lived in a huge tent with three rooms. My earliest memory is of my mother, during the two-month rainy season which we had each year, leaning over me and asking, Are you warm enough? before laying another coat on the bed.

At about the same time that D and her family were leaving Odessa in 1917, the forty-three-year-old Chaim Weizmann was consolidating his place in the hearts and minds of the British people, partly by his professional contributions to the munitions industry and partly by his highly articulate presentation of the Zionist cause. When the Prime Minister, David Lloyd George, asked him to consider ways in which Britain might show her gratitude to him for his help with the war effort, Weizmann took the opportunity to promote Zionism and his hopes for a Jewish homeland. The British Government responded in November with the so-called Balfour Declaration. In it, Lord Balfour, the Foreign Secretary, outlined Britain's support for the development of a Jewish homeland in Palestine, with the proviso that this should not "prejudice the rights of existing non-Jewish communities". The rider was inserted in order to satisfy the local Arab community, which had occupied the area for centuries.

Throughout the world, Jews rejoiced as they heard the news. In the synagogues, prayers of thanks were offered that the promises made in the Bible of an end to exile and the "Return to Zion" were at last about to be fulfilled. But Zionism was also now seen in British political circles as a useful force that could support the Allied cause. Appealing to Zionists in Russia might help prevent the withdrawal of that country from the war. In the United States, Zionists could be enlisted to convince the Americans that their contribution was vital, now that they had at last declared their intention to enter the war. David Ben-Gurion, who had lived in Palestine since 1906 and formed the first Jewish trade union there in 1915, was now in the States, having been expelled from Palestine by the Turks for expressing pro-Allied sympathies. Ben-Gurion was busy helping to raise the Jewish Legion and now, armed with the support of Great Britain, he made his way to the White House, where he enlisted the support of President Woodrow Wilson for the Legion. Wilson drew the line, however, at Ben-Gurion's suggestion that the Legion be used to drive the Turks from Palestine. The United States was officially at war with Germany, not with Turkey. But Wilson pointed out that Ben-Gurion could discuss the idea with the British, who were fighting both countries.

In London, the War Office treated Ben-Gurion's proposal with initial suspicion: the idea of a trained military Zionist force in possession of Palestine carried overtones of an army of occupation which, once installed, might not wish to leave. However, such reservations were ultimately overcome and, with the help of both the British and the US Governments, the Zionists began to enlist young Jews into a special unit of the British Army which would serve in the Middle East.

From the Allied point of view, any action in which the enemy could be engaged without deploying their own existing forces would benefit the cause. The Sinai Desert was a vast area which would have to be covered if the Allies were to run the Turks out of Palestine, so the undertaking which faced the Jewish Legion was no mean one. Those Jews enlisting in the Allied forces were told by their draft boards that if they wished to transfer to the Jewish Legion they were at liberty to do so. Thousands took up the offer and were soon serving under their own banner, having taken the ancient oath of loyalty, "May my right hand lose its cunning if I forget thee, O Jerusalem." Ben-Gurion himself served with them.

Under their own Jewish commanders, they followed Field Marshal Viscount Edmund Allenby as he made his way through Gaza and Beersheba, and they took the city of Jerusalem from the Turks on 11 December 1917. After 400 years of occupation, the Turkish rule in Palestine was over. Eleven months later to the day, the Great War itself came to an end.

As leader of the Zionist Commission to Palestine, Chaim Weizmann now felt the time was ripe to implement the Balfour Declaration. It was one thing for the British to incline towards support and understanding for the Jewish position in Palestine on paper; now the moment had come to put theory into practice. It was also important to convince the Arabs that the Declaration was in the interests of their people, too. Weizmann entered into talks with Emir Feisal, the third son of the Sherif of Mecca (modern Saudi Arabia) and leader, alongside T. E. Lawrence, of the Arab revolt against the Turks. They discussed ways of making the British plan acceptable to the Arab nation. Feisal was in favour of the idea at first, as it emerged that he was under the impression that the incoming Jews would be bringing with them great wealth which the Arab aristocracy might be able to exploit; but once disabused of this, the Emir did a *volte face* and flatly refused to consider Palestine as an area available for Jewish colonisation.

The socialist-leaning leaders of the Zionist movement may have sympathised with Arab concern about being displaced by Jewish immigrants, but their own history taught them that they also had a right to settle in a country which formed such a fundamental part of their heritage. Furthermore, their dream of a land of their own seemed to be within their grasp and they were not about to turn back now. Having received the British diplomatic backing which was so important to their cause, they were determined to push on with their plans to open Palestine to any Jews who wished to settle there, and perhaps especially to those who were seeking a haven from persecution.

With the war over, the Balfour Declaration had given Zionism a new status in British political thinking. After four centuries the Turks were gone, leaving Palestine with the possibility of a peaceful future, if only the Arab and Jewish inhabitants could work side by side to rebuild a country which had suffered so greatly. The Jews of Palestine had survived a cruel war. Disease and famine had reduced their population from 100,000 to a mere 55,000. The Turkish occupiers, aware of the pro-British sympathies of the local population, had executed hundreds as "spies". The survivors had kept going through the generosity of overseas subsidies, but now the barren, cracked earth needed farmers to tend it and irrigation to combat the unforgiving sun. The war had brought an end to the export of commodities such as wine and oranges, and now the vineyards and the citrus groves were dying of neglect.

The great peace conference to sort out the future of Europe in the wake of the First World War was convened at Paris on 18 January 1919. It was to last almost exactly a year. Among the many issues debated was the future of Palestine. When Chaim Weizmann made his deliberate way to the podium on the day he was due to speak, Jews waited anxiously to hear what he was going to say. Might it be that Weizmann was the one who at last had an answer to the age-old "Jewish Question"?

Although no direct answer was forthcoming – and indeed how could one be after so many centuries of Diaspora, and a homeland occupied since the days of Alexander the Great? – the words Weizmann spoke reminded all who listened to them of the ancient history of the Jews. Palestine had been part of that history for 4,000 years; it had never ceased to be the homeland and now it was crying out to all Jews willing to settle there.

There was nothing new in this, to be sure; but people sat forward on their seats when Weizmann began to outline, for the first time ever, the idea of an immigration programme under

Zionist management which would aim to send between 70,000 and 80,000 thousand immigrants to Palestine each year and "make Palestine as Jewish as America is American or England English".

The idea was greeted enthusiastically by many, though by no means all. However, prodded by the American President, Woodrow Wilson, the Paris Conference endorsed the principle of self-determination for the Jews and laid the foundations for the formal incorporation of the Balfour Declaration in the League of Nations Mandate for Palestine, which was officially granted to Britain at the San Remo Conference in 1920.

But not all those present at the Paris Peace Conference were happy about the idea of tens of thousands of Jews heading for Palestine on a regular basis. One British official objected to the phrasing of one of the minutes, "recognising the historic connection of the Jewish People with Palestine". Stressing that his was a personal opinion, he remarked, "I do not myself recognise that the connection of the Jews with Palestine, which terminated 1,200 years ago, gives them any claim whatsoever."

There were many in the Arab community in Palestine who agreed with him. After Arab riots in Jerusalem intensified, an indication of the troubled times that lay ahead, the British decided to have a stab at coming up with a resolution to the conflict of interests. The first step was to send a representative who would be in a position to observe the situation. The man they chose was Sir Herbert Samuel, a Jew and a Zionist, who was the first British High Commissioner for Palestine.

With such a background, Samuel might not have been expected to be impartial but, much to the disappointment of the Palestine Jews, the new arrival followed the official British line and supported the appointment of a leading agitator and member of the Arab community, Haj Mohammed Amin el Husseini, to the important position of Grand Mufti of Jerusalem. The Jews were further angered by the British decision to make the Hashemite Emir Abdullah, an ally in the war, ruler of Transjordan, a newly created semi-autonomous kingdom, thereby slicing from the Palestine Mandate all the land east of the River Jordan. By this action, Palestine was divided into two domains. Although the area west of the River Jordan was retained as Jewish Palestine, Jews were prohibited from settling in Transjordan or owning property there. However, Arab settlements in Jewish Palestine remained.

What had appeared to the British as an ideal plan on paper – a judicious division of the available land between Jew and Arab – in practice was a disaster. The British may have been happy with the division: those who lived in Palestine were not. The Jews felt that the part they were cut off from was as much a part of their heritage as the western coastal plain. The Arabs felt that to surrender any of their territory to what they saw as Jewish intruders did not constitute a solution to any problem at all. Once again Britain had sliced up land with no reference to the culture, politics or history of those who lived there. The two sides glared at one another across the imposed divide.

Chapter Three:
A Question of Ownership

The British Empire had once more proudly entered a country with military bands playing "God Save the King" to stir the hearts of the troops; but the end of the First World War had left Britain in charge of a place of which they knew very little indeed. Who actually owned the land, and where exactly were the historical borders? It was true that Palestine was apparently naturally divided by the River Jordan, but where did the Sinai Peninsula to the south, and Syria and Lebanon to the north, fit in? Most of the borders had changed and changed again with the passing of the centuries, and it was not easy to decide where the country began and where it ended.

Feeling his way through a tangle of conflicting opinions, in 1922 the then Colonial Secretary, Winston Churchill, published a White Paper. Intended as a compromise, it managed to be sympathetic to the Jews while at the same time reassuring the Arabs regarding their concerns about the presumed flood of immigrants. The British Government would allow the further development of a Jewish community in Palestine; but it would control the number of settlers to ensure that immigration would not swamp the economic resources of the country. The British knew that whatever decision they made would have its critics, but they felt they could at least congratulate themselves that they had paid attention to the views of both sides.

The number of deaths and the amount of devastation in the First World War caused mankind to reflect on its capacity for destruction. In 1919, Woodrow Wilson tabled the idea of a League of Nations which would work together to prevent the recurrence of such horrors, and on 10 January 1920 the League became a reality. With fifty-two nations agreeing that there was a historical connection between the Jews and Palestine, Zionists began to feel an increased optimism for their cause; but the League went no further in its support. The British were the ones who had successfully overrun Palestine. The British were the authors of the Balfour Declaration. The British had wide administrative experience in the Middle East. Therefore the management of Palestine had better be left to Britain.

The League instructed Britain to "facilitate" Jewish immigration into Palestine and to encourage Jews to develop the land which now lay barren in so many areas. The official languages of Palestine would be Arabic, English and Hebrew, and, for the first time, the Zionist Organisation was officially instructed to help Britain administer Jewish affairs in Palestine.

There was no question about where the Zionists' sympathies lay. The organisation had gained strength among the restive Jewish masses of Eastern Europe, who wanted nothing more than the right to return to what they saw as their ancestral home. Meanwhile, in the USA, both houses of Congress unanimously approved the League's instructions and issued a statement of support signed by President Wilson himself. Even the Emir Feisal now issued a statement of support, in which he said, "We feel that the Arabs and the Jews are cousins in race, having suffered similar oppressions at the hands of powers stronger than ourselves."

The words had been easy to deliver. Putting them into an action which would solve the problems now existing in Palestine would not be so easy.

The rest of the world may have been quick to make suggestions, but the answer to the riddle posed by these two peoples remained one that Britain had to solve. Governing a country like Palestine was fine if everyone was prepared to abide by the rules and live peacefully together. If this were not possible, then other measures would have to be taken.

Meanwhile, the Jews and the Arabs of Palestine had their own pressing local problems to contend with. Jews were pouring into the country from all over the world and needed some common cause to unite them. Ben-Gurion, with his genius for leadership, aimed to promulgate the idea of a future self-governing Jewish state built and based on a unified working class. Within a few years, he managed to create a general federation of labour, called Histadrut. With Ben-Gurion as its chief secretary, the federation swiftly set about building blocks of flats, schools, agricultural villages, a bank and a theatre.

Britain, undaunted by the apparently insurmountable problem it faced, began to bring together representatives from the Jewish Agency and the leadership of the Palestine Arabs. It was no surprise, however, that the two sides were divided on almost every issue. What complicated matters further was that each side had a certain amount of justification in whatever stance it took. Throughout their history, the Arabs of the area had known no other home. They were in the majority and wanted to remain so. Despite their poverty and their simple agricultural existence, they were quite content for things to remain as they were. But the Jews could also trace their roots in Palestine back thousands of years. They wanted to bring more and more people in, and they wanted to develop the land.

There was something else: whatever reservations were being expressed around the world about the viability of the "Zionist enterprise" in Palestine, thousands of Jews were ignoring them, and, as they saw it, coming home.

Chapter Four:
A Land Looking for People

Although so many Jews worldwide had answered the Zionist call, Palestine was still underpopulated, and from London's point of view there was no reason not to encourage settlers to come to this backward and run-down corner of the world. And what better settlers than the Jews? As a people, they had the ability and courage needed to work the undeveloped desert land. If anyone could make it bloom, they could. One only had to look at what had already been accomplished. With fewer than 100,000 immigrants, green and fertile fields were already emerging in the neglected valleys, and land that had been nothing but malarial swamp was now drained and dotted with clean white villages. The Jews had the ability to create wealth which would benefit both themselves and the Arabs. Why not let them try?

Perez Leshem, born in Germany, was ready to answer the call. He had been a clerk in a large Jewish factory before deciding to study agriculture and emigrate to Palestine. His wife by his side, Leshem set out on the great adventure:

My parents were members of a large Jewish organisation; but you must understand that I belonged to a generation which was very much influenced by the First World War and the troubles that immediately followed it – the revolution in Russia and all the upheavals in Central

Europe. At the time there were many Orthodox Jews coming into Germany from Poland.

I became a Zionist, and left home for a small town in southern Germany, where I studied agriculture and learned such practical skills as milking cows. Later, armed with my new knowledge, I went on to Berlin University. By the winter of 1925, I had decided that the time had come to leave for Palestine.

My wife and I travelled first to her parents' home in Munich, and from there we went on to Venice and thence to Trieste. In Trieste we boarded a cargo boat bound for Jaffa. We were the only passengers. The journey took eight days. When we arrived in Jaffa, we found it to be a very different place from anywhere we had known in Europe. It was very small, and the people seemed noisy and uncultivated – in great contrast to what we had known in Germany.

However important a facet of life an indigenous culture may be for most countries, the fact that people from all sorts of different backgrounds, nationalities and walks of life could come together in Palestine and gradually work to create, as if by magic, a new unity that showed itself in all aspects of daily life, was something which impressed Hayim Hefer when he arrived:

The German Jews did a lot for the country. Take the coffee shops, for example. The Polish Jews had never seen a coffee shop. The thought of sitting outside, idly drinking coffee and talking, was something quite alien to the Polish mind. The Poles would have been quite happy scoffing a hamburger or maybe some sausage – that was OK because you could do it fast. There never seemed to be enough time for the Polish Jews. The German Jews enjoyed whiling their time away, though they brought us more than coffee shops: with them came the development of industry and the building of synagogues; there was an important newspaper which was owned by a German Jew; and among them you could find any number of doctors, professors and scientists.

Although people were anxious to reach Palestine, travelling in the 1920s was a far cry from what it is today. Perez Leshem and his wife left Jaffa to join a kibbutz:

We went by train from Jaffa to Tel Aviv, and from there on to the kibbutz by agricultural wagon. The whole journey took us twelve hours. Today it would take one hour by car – but I think there were only ten cars in the whole of Palestine in those days.

There were about fifty or fifty-five people on the kibbutz. All we had for shelter were a few tents and a small cowshed. We did whatever kind of work was required. We just got on with it. The work we did was very primitive and there was no irrigation then. Most of us suffered from malaria. But we were determined to make the kibbutz a success through our efforts, and a place for other Jews who would come after us. Our job was to create a Jewish homeland.

Like Leshem, many of the new settlers adopted the kibbutz way of life. The idea of the kibbutz was introduced to the country at the turn of the century. Groups of young farmers needing help in coming to terms with the harsh land had banded together and devised a masterly plan: each new settlement would be a commune. The children studied together, ate together and slept in dormitories. The families worked as one, and had all their goods and farm implements in common. So successful was the kibbutz idea that it is seen as a principal reason for the remarkable success that the Jews had in taming the land. Not surprisingly, the kibbutz remains a major way of life in Israel to this day.

Jewish Palestine was fortunate in the diverse expertise and culture immigrants brought with them. Hayim Hefer remembers:

Not far from Tel Aviv was a village settlement that had been built by German Jews. It was fantastic. There were three-year-olds there, singing Mozart and playing Schubert. It was an absolute pinnacle of culture.

But there were problems. Hefer adds:

One of the biggest challenges facing the new country was communication. The immigrants who came pouring in were from all the four corners of the world. It was like the Tower of Babel: Palestine was suddenly filled with people speaking dozens of different languages, and all of us trying to understand each other.

What was the point of building a new nation if the members of your new society were unable to communicate with one another? To Ben-Gurion's way of thinking, there was only one language that would unite the Jewish people, and that was Hebrew. Hayim Hefer knew this before he arrived – he'd been warned before his departure that the most difficult problem he would face would be that of communication:

> Although we did not speak Hebrew, we came anyway, fully intending to learn the language when we arrived. We certainly knew that we would not be alone. I knew Russian speakers and French speakers; and the Jews from the Yemen spoke Arabic. The Jews of Central Europe spoke Yiddish.
>
> But the miracle was that after a while, all the people had learned Hebrew. And they spoke it in every field – physics, psychology, you name it. But the environment played an important part in learning the language. You could point to various things in the landscape and try to give them a Hebrew name.
>
> There were difficulties, though. Heres an example: sixty or seventy years ago there were no Hebrew words for the different kinds of flower. They used to say "kind of a tree" or "kind of a flower" – something like that. Contrast that with Arabic, where there are several words just for a camel.
>
> At first it was hard to encourage people to speak Hebrew. What do you do with a language that has no word for a telephone? But we needed a common language and to a certain extent we had to develop what was missing in pure Hebrew from our own resources. As I've said, the environment presented a challenge; but we also needed to know how to curse. Who can talk without being able to swear? And, as in the course of time words were invented to fulfil other needs, so we developed swear words. Russian and Arabic both have a rich supply of them, so we weren't short of raw material. The first people to invent curses were the farmers and the market vendors. Suddenly you heard these new words and you asked yourself, "What's that? What does it mean?"
>
> You can gauge the strength of a group or a tribe by their sensitivity to jokes made at their expense. The Moroccans are prickly. The Jews are prickly. But the Russian Jews didn't care. One of the papers carried an advert calling for new Russian girls. If the ad had been for new

Moroccan girls, the paper would have been burned. But gradually
we found our way to a sense of unity, and it was one of the big
success stories of the Jews who came to Palestine, that they were all
able to adapt to a new common language.

   Initially there was a big battle, if you like, between Hebrew and
Yiddish. The first ones to arrive spoke Yiddish, and so many Jews
speak Yiddish that for a time it looked as if Yiddish would win the
day. I mean, why learn a new language if you've already got one
that a lot of you have in common? But Hebrew was our language,
the language of the new country, with no associations other than
with Israel.

Hebrew was not an easy language to learn, however. Percy
Manham, who came to Palestine from South Africa, finds it
a challenge to this day:

The greatest disappointment in my life has been my lack of Hebrew.
I have not been able to master it. When I was a youngster, I had the
same trouble trying to learn Afrikaans. When I arrived in Palestine,
my Granny and I went to a private teacher. I would go in the mornings
from 7.30 to 8.30, and from the lesson on to the office. But as soon
as I arrived in the office, all I had learned was forgotten.

Everyone tried to overcome the problem presented by speaking
Hebrew in his or her own way. Hayim Hefer remembers:

I've told you about this extremely successful village of German settlers
not far from Tel Aviv. They decided that as they were Zionists,
they would set aside one day a week when no one was to speak
German. They would only speak Hebrew. It was the quietest day of
the week.

The task which now faced Ben-Gurion was to persuade the
older and senior members of society to allow themselves to
be open to the ideas and influences of the newer and younger
arrivals in Palestine. It was not an easy job; while Ben-Gurion
managed to bring most of the Jewish leadership round to his
way of thinking, he fared less well with senior Arabs, who
saw few advantages in the changes. There was, however, an

exception to this reaction among those Arabs who lived close to Jewish settlements: they quickly realised that their lives need not remain rooted in past traditions. A way of improving their standard of living had arrived from outside and they were quite prepared to learn and adopt the ways of the Jewish settlers. After all, what was wrong with having a separate shed for your goat and your donkey? And why not irrigate their fields, as the Jews were doing, and grow some vegetables?

Just as these changes were being made in the rural areas, so life in the towns was also beginning to improve. New industries appeared. Cement factories, power plants and road-building started to provide jobs not only for urban Jews, but for urban Arabs as well. No longer, in fact, were the Arabs condemned to a life of dismal resentment. They suddenly discovered that their standard of living had become far higher than that of Arabs in neighbouring countries. Word spread, and before long an Arab immigration began, as people packed their bags and brought their families to a country which promised so much better a way of life. Between 1922 and 1925, almost 30,000 Arabs came into Palestine from Syria, Transjordan and Iraq. Many saw Palestine as a place to get temporary work, by which means they could save enough to pay off family debts or buy land back home. Thousands took jobs with the British Mandatory Government. For the first time it could be shown that it was possible for Arab and Jew to live side by side and prosper in peace.

Chapter Five: Hostilities

Not everyone was happy with these changes. Many of the Arab landowners were furious at the latest developments – they felt that any improvement in the lot of the average Arab would undermine their power and authority. Peasants were simply peasants, and God had willed that they should remain so. In the landowners' eyes, God had also willed that they should remain the masters. They decided to exploit the religious fervour of the peasantry as a means of redressing the balance and of appeasing their own feelings of discontent. It was not long before there was a shift in Arab attitudes: Arabs began to view Jews no longer as benefactors, but as unwelcome invaders who were reaping the benefits of a country which was not rightfully theirs.

Old hatreds surfaced and expressed themselves in violence. One atrocity saw forty new immigrants murdered and mutilated. Gangs of Arab youths ran amok in the streets of Jerusalem, and Jews were murdered and raped in the Old City. The settlements in Upper Galilee fared no better: they became a favourite target and, although Ben-Gurion did his best to continue to offer the hand of peace to the Arabs, begging them to carry on living in peace beside their Jewish fellow-workers, the violence escalated.

Despite the hostility, however, the population continued to grow. Row upon row of pretty little houses began to spring up in Tel Aviv. Camels and donkeys carried bags of sand from the seashore to the building sites along paved streets lined with trees. Riots in the port of Jaffa nearby had encouraged an increasing number of Jews to move to Tel Aviv, even though there was as yet no proper accommodation for them and they were forced to live in huts and tents. And still wave upon wave of new immigrants arrived.

The majority of the newcomers were labourers. Their arrival meant that membership of Ben-Gurion's General Federation of Labour increased to over 4,000. Small factories began to spring up. Tel Aviv was only twelve years old, yet it was already well on the way to becoming a major metropolis. There was now an all-Jewish police force, and a high school was built – the first truly imposing civic building, past which small buses and horse-drawn carriages – as yet the only forms of transport – trundled.

Since 1919, both the Jewish and the Arab populations had grown steadily. The number of Jews had risen from 55,000 to 162,000; but the number of Arabs had grown by 500 per cent to 800,000 – an increase mainly due to large families and improved living conditions, as well as greatly improved sanitation and health, for which both the British and the Jewish authorities could claim credit. The British had worked wonders by draining the malarial swamps and thus reducing the death rate. They had also built schools and improved the quality of farm livestock. A network of roads across the country made communications easier and benefited everyone.

But as the country took shape, nationalistic sentiments among both Arabs and Jews became increasingly entrenched. On the Arab side, the nationalism was promoted by agitators working for the Mufti, who encouraged their people to riot against the so-called newcomers: their hostility was directed at the Jews and the British in equal measure. All the most influential political and administrative positions were held by British officials; only the lowlier places were occupied by Jews or Arabs. As bitterness grew, so the Arabs saw the answer to their perceived problem as a simple one, and the talk in the coffee houses revolved around two questions: how to get the whole of their land back and how to get rid of the Jews.

David Bar-Illan, advisor to the present Israeli Prime Minister, remembers how dangerous it was for his mother at that time. She had opened the first dress shop in Haifa and was determined to stay in Palestine. In the face of the constant threat of Arab attacks, she was ready to defend herself, and others, if the need arose:

> When she was pregnant with me, she was able to smuggle hand grenades in pockets that she had sewn into her dress. With these she was quite prepared to help defend the Jewish community in Haifa. Being pregnant meant that it was easier to conceal the grenades.

The Arab attacks were of grave concern, but they did not prevent the progress that continued to be made. Having presided over the beginning of the process, the British Mandatory Government was happy to transfer some of its power, allowing the Jews to levy their own taxes on buildings and to manage their own water system.

Palestine was becoming more sophisticated with every year that passed, but there was still a long way to go, and the cultural and physical shock for the newly arrived immigrant could be considerable. During the summer months the heat was oppressive and unrelieved, and flies swarmed everywhere. In Jerusalem, stray cats wandered the streets in such large numbers that people had to put wire mesh across their windows to prevent them from coming into their houses. A true Israeli state was still in the future and there was no Ministry of Absorption to deal with the newcomers. Those who arrived without friends to greet them found it especially difficult; the more so since most of the existing settlers felt that the new ones should do as they had done, and find their feet without help. In any case, no agencies yet existed to do that job for them.

Some of the newcomers, like Jona Rosenfeld, travelled in style – Jona was fortunate enough to have had a berth on a cruise ship. But disembarkation carried the usual rude shocks with it:

> We arrived in Haifa on a terribly hot day and had to wait in the sun. Immigration took ages – not out of nastiness, but inefficiency. It took almost ten hours for them to clear us. I remember feeling sure that we would never get off that boat. I was very worried about a devout Jew who was so concerned about missing *shul* that he kept running from one deck to another, trying to find the shortest queue

and shouting all the time. I was just a child then. I couldn't figure out what was going on.

Later, we met up with my father and my brother, who were already there, waiting for us. We left the next day by bus and went to Jerusalem via Tel Aviv. It was an awful journey. The bus was packed and the weather was boiling.

Many of the new immigrants had similar experiences, but the satisfaction and pleasure they felt when they suddenly found themselves surrounded by people of their own faith far out-weighed the difficulties they had to overcome. Never before had they been driven by a Jewish bus-driver; the landlady who took their rent was Jewish; the people who ran the corner shop were Jews. All around were their own people – a constant reminder that at last they were living in a homeland of their own.

But all these new people needed space to live. The Jewish National Fund, created in 1901, had managed to purchase large parcels of land from Arab owners at generous prices for this purpose. Those who benefited remembered with gratitude the small tin collection boxes placed beside the Sabbath candles in the synagogues of their distant home towns. The fund had been started by the Zionist movement with the exclusive aim of gathering capital with which to buy and develop land in Palestine. Arab landowners who dealt with the fund – many of them based in Amman, Damascus and Beirut – became very rich indeed, selling land for which they had no use, land which frequently comprised nothing more than deadly swamps where the risk of catching malaria or blackwater fever was high.

Having bought such poisonous ground, there remained the task of bringing it under cultivation. Few farmers would even think about such Herculean labour, but a group existed which was specially prepared to take on the exhausting and dangerous work. The Labour Zionist Movement was made up of highly motivated pioneers – *halutzim* – who were ready to throw themselves at any job which would reclaim the land for the future of their country. So dedicated to their cause were they that they excluded Arabs from working alongside them. Only Jewish workers could be permitted to create the homeland. The Emek Swamps, drained by these remarkable people and turned into gardens which occupy one of the most beautiful and fertile valleys in the whole of Israel, are their greatest monument.

And still Jews continued to pour into the country – far more than there was work for. For these newcomers, the conflict with the Arabs was overshadowed by the need to find employment. Of the Jewish population of Palestine in 1927, 7,000 were without work. Not surprisingly, many became disillusioned and, after trying their best to settle down, gave up the struggle and made their way to the United States, or to countries which formed part of the British Empire. No immigrants from the USSR returned there: to have done so would have meant death, or at the very least exile in the barren wastes of Siberia.

The reasons for the lack of work were manifold. For one thing, the economy of Palestine was still in a very primitive state. With the exception of the building industry, which employed half the workforce, there were no large employers and there was not enough capital to create further work opportunities. Then there was competition for the jobs that did exist. Wages for Jewish workers were low, and lower still for Arabs. This meant that Jewish orange growers, for example, employed Arab labourers, because it made better economic sense to do so.

But the tensions between Arab and Jew did not go away, and by 1929 Arab rioting had increased to so great an extent that the British authorities were obliged to intervene. The solution, as they saw it, was simple. The Arabs were unhappy because there were too many Jews. If immigration ceased or was at least severely limited, the Arabs would be mollified and life in Palestine could return to normal.

The Jews, however, had not forgotten the Balfour Declaration, and especially not its opening words: "His Majesty's Government view with favour the establishment in Palestine of a national home for the Jewish people, and will use their best endeavours to facilitate the achievement of this object . . ." Even though the Declaration continued, ". . . it being clearly understood that nothing shall be done which may prejudice the civil and religious rights of existing non-Jewish communities in Palestine . . .", there was no question that the Jews would not take lightly any interference in their hard-won achievements now.

Chapter Six: Staying On

The Arab leaders were prepared to do everything possible to get the Jews out of Palestine. Although opinions in the Jewish community on how to combat this attitude were divided, a militia was established which went by the name of Haganah – the Hebrew for "self-defence". The Haganah was a secret organisation the precise nature of which is difficult to define. Sometimes it went underground completely, when it was harassed by the Mandatory Authority; at other times, it was recognised by the British as a quasi-official force.

The Haganah was conceived literally as a defence force: its stance was non-aggressive. In this way, the Palestine Jews felt that they were not doing anything to upset the British, who might put an end to the immigration quotas at any time. However, the series of atrocities in 1929 revealed the weaknesses of the Haganah. The men who served in it were poorly trained, under-equipped and badly organised. Apart from guard duties in Jewish settlements, its effect was limited.

The Jews were quick to learn the lesson of this experience, and again opinion divided. Some continued to favour a policy of non-violence; others felt that the Haganah should be built up into an armed force capable of giving as good as it got – there seemed to be little point in passively waiting for Arab attacks and then putting up with them. By 1931, plans to develop the Haganah were under way.

It was the British, though, who first took a hard line with the terrorists. General John Dill, a tough British officer who took a disinterested view of Palestine's internal affairs, started a policy of stiff fines or immediate arrest for those involved in any acts of aggression – whether Arab or Jew. Curfews were imposed and if a terrorist was caught in hiding, the house of the person sheltering him was destroyed. As a result of Dill's work, the unrest quickly died down. His approach was an inspiration to the Haganah leadership. If the British could be tough with the Arabs – and the Arabs, being the more aggressive side, bore the brunt of Dill's severity – and it worked, then perhaps the Jews could go on the offensive and fight for their land. The question which divided the leadership was how far to go. Inevitably, the group splintered and a more aggressive Haganah B force was formed, called Irgun Zvai Leumi-Etzel. One of its later leaders was an immigrant Polish Jew called Menachem Begin, who was to become a hawkish prime minister of Israel in the mid-1970s.

Another member of the group who was destined to lead his country was Yitzhak Shamir. He was still a schoolboy when he decided to join the underground force:

> I remember that the ceremony took place in a Tel Aviv schoolroom. Since the schools were closed in the afternoons and opened again in the evenings it was a perfect place to use when the underground wanted to do any training. The classroom was dark when I was led in. A bright light shone into my eyes, so that I could not see the three men sitting behind the table. These were the members of the committee who interviewed any prospective member. They asked me many things; whether I was willing to accept orders, whether I was prepared to make sacrifices. They told me that if I joined I would be in great danger, and asked me if that bothered me. I said that it didn't. They seemed satisfied and then they asked me to repeat the oath of allegiance to the Irgun. I knew before I entered the room that I would be accepted. I still remember the oath: We swear allegiance to the Irgun Zvai Leumi in the Land of Israel. We shall be ready at any time to act in the cause of the rebirth of the nation of Israel in its homeland. To live and die for it.

As we have seen, tension between the Arabs and the Jews had steadily increased during the latter half of the 1920s. The Arab side had stepped up their campaign of violence as their determination to drive the Jews out grew greater, and as it became apparent that the Jews were not easily intimidated. But the Jews were capable of inflammatory actions too. In 1928, a group of Ultra-Orthodox Jews set up a screen to separate men and women at prayer at the Wailing Wall in Jerusalem. They erected the screen in an area which the Arabs considered historically to be theirs. In August 1929, the British police removed the screen, but that led only to more riots and outbreaks of violence between the two sides. The divide – as subsequent history has shown – was rapidly becoming unbridgeable. The British had developed roads within the country and helped with agricultural and health improvements and reform; but they had not invested as much in the development of the economy as the Jews, and although they were officially in control of the country, they did little to ease the tension.

It is hard to see what they could have done, as matters were fast getting out of control; certainly the fact that they took sides with the Mufti and curtailed the Jewish immigration quota didn't help. By 1930, the British were threatening to put an end to Jewish immigration completely; but it should be remembered that the Jewish population was growing more quickly than there were jobs or than the economy could support, and that the Balfour Declaration's intention was to aid Jews without detriment to the indigenous Arab population. Britain's real mistake, as usual, was to make lordly commitments before it had done its homework properly. The Arabs, not without justification, felt that the deluge of Jewish immigrants was an infringement of their rights in Palestine, and invoked that part of the Balfour Declaration which favoured them. The British, uncomfortable with the worsening situation, placed the blame firmly in the camp of the Jews, who they felt were encouraging immigration and, by so doing, provoking the increased tension between the two groups.

The riots of 1929 had settled nothing, although they left 133 dead and 399 wounded on the Jewish side – all at the hands of the Arabs – and 78 Arabs dead and scores of others wounded, mostly in clashes with British forces. Time passed, and for a while the international press shifted its interest, but the threat of violence in Palestine was never far from the surface and the Jews continued to live in a state of emergency. Arab hatred hung in the air like a shroud.

The hatred exploded again in Jaffa in April 1930. Sixteen Jews were killed by Arab gangs. The violence quickly spread to Jerusalem, where a Jewish merchant was beaten up and left for dead in the Old City. These actions led to the establishment of the Arab Strike Committee, supported by the Mufti, which called on all Arab merchants to close their shops and businesses in protest at continued Jewish immigration. Quite a number of Arab businessmen ignored this behest, being perfectly happy to keep their doors open to anyone who came to them with money; nor were they intimidated by the gangs of Arab youths who came round to "request" them to pay attention to the Strike Committee's demands.

The Mufti escalated his campaign, first issuing a decree that no Arab would pay tax until the British stopped selling land to the Jews (which seemed an odd notion, considering that so many Arabs had done so). Then he inaugurated an Arab National Government, to which the Jews responded with Jerusalem Radio. The British High Commissioner finally announced that the Mandatory Government would "suppress all outbreaks of lawlessness and punish the perpetrators"; but the effect of this threat was minimal. At midnight following the announcement an Arab watchman, quietly doing his job at a Jewish-owned quarry, was shot dead by fellow Arabs: he had refused to leave his post and join the strike.

More killings followed within weeks. In the Jewish Quarter of Jerusalem two Jews were gunned down; one of them, a forty-six-year-old rabbi called Reuben Kloppholtz, left a wife and eight children. The other was an elderly Jew who lived in a nearby old people's home – he was shot through the mouth. The Mufti's response to these deaths took the form of a statement in which he repeated the theme that the Jews were trying to take over the country and in so doing "murdering our sons and burning our houses".

The Arab terror campaign continued. A gunman burst into

the Edison Film Theatre in Jerusalem and opened fire on the audience. Three people died: one, Dr Zvi Szabchoski, was a dermatologist who had arrived in the country from Poland only three months earlier; Alexandra Polonsky, also from Poland and a recent immigrant, was a student at the Hebrew University; the third was a baker who had celebrated his marriage only three weeks before. Their funerals took place the following day and resulted in a remarkable show of defiance from the Jewish settlers. Business in the Jewish Quarter came to a standstill as staff left offices and shops to attend the funerals and pay their respects. More than 10,000 mourners stood to listen to the Chairman of the General Council of Palestine Jews, Yitzhak Ben-Zvi, who told them, "This crime in the midst of the Jewish sector of Jerusalem, committed in such a strikingly bold manner, has aroused an unprecedented uproar among the Jews."

These killings did not provoke a violent response from the Jews, but the Arab attacks continued and soon three more people were killed. The staff and students of the Mount Scopus campus of the Hebrew University felt especially vulnerable, the more so when a staff member, Lewis Billig, was murdered at his desk in the small suburb of North Talpiot. This was an especially tragic death, as the young English academic was a firm believer in the possibility of Arabs and Jews living peacefully and happily together. The key to this, he felt, lay in an understanding of each other's history and culture. At the time of his death he was preparing an edition of a ninth-century Arab text.

None of these events weakened the resolve of the Jewish leadership. Palestine was their rightful home. The doors would remain open to as many new settlers as wanted to come. Room for them to live, and work for them to do, would be found and created.

Meanwhile the British continued to try to find ways out of the maze. A Commission of Enquiry was set up under Sir Walter Shaw and reported unsurprisingly that Zionist requests for increased immigration quotas were one of the principal matters for concern among the Arab population. To this Sir John Simpson replied that there would soon not be enough land in Palestine to provide the Arabs with a healthy livelihood. He therefore proposed that Jewish immigration be suspended. A Zionist lobby immediately set to work against this proposal and quickly succeeded in putting a strain on Anglo-US relations. The USA, which even before the Second World War had a huge Jewish population, espoused the interests of the Palestine Jews. In February 1931, the British Prime Minister, Ramsay Macdonald, sent a letter to Chaim Weizmann. He assured the Zionist leader that Britain had every intention of upholding the policy of supporting the Jewish national home and that he had no plans to break the British Government's agreement with and obligation to world Jewry. The letter to Weizmann was rejected by the Arabs, who promptly gave it a nickname – "The Black Letter".

But events were occurring in Europe which would soon overshadow the internal affairs of Palestine and affect the future of the little country fundamentally and forever. In Germany, the Weimar Republic, which had bravely kept going since the end of the First World War as the country's first experiment with real democracy, was tottering to its close. In its place loomed a new militarism and a new absolutism; a small, new political party was gaining ever greater control and would soon form a government which would hurl the world into chaos and change the face of Europe forever. The National Socialist German Workers' Party had a leader called Adolf Hitler, who had two main ambitions: world domination and the expulsion of the Jews from all the territories he controlled. And if no one would take them, they would have to be destroyed.

Chapter Seven: Driven by Hate

Up until the 1930s, immigrants had been coming to Palestine from all over the world. Now, the focus was to sharpen on Europe.

Anti-Semitism in Europe could be traced back to the earliest, ancient Jewish settlements. Examples of pogroms and ghettos can be found as long ago as the early Middle Ages, and in the fourteenth century the Jews were blamed for the Great Plague, even though as many Jews died of it as did the rest of the population of Europe. The nineteenth century saw a rebirth of anti-Semitism in Russia and eastern Europe, and many Jews fled into western Europe or emigrated to America and Palestine as a result. Hitler, who fed on such poisonous anti-Semitic publications as *The Protocols of the Elders of Zion* and Houston Stewart Chamberlain's *The Foundations of the Nineteenth Century*, saw in the Jews a focus for all his frustration, envy and hate; but when he chose them as a scapegoat for Germany's ills, he found that most people were willing to follow his lead. The Gentiles of Austria and Poland, indeed, were more enthusiastic anti-Semites even than the Germans, as were the Latvians, Lithuanians and Ukrainians. Poland, where the worst concentration camps and all the death camps were located, had a huge Jewish community – 3,300,000, ten per cent of the population, and the second largest group in the Diaspora. Of these, 2,800,000 were killed. Today, there are about 5,000 Jews in the country, most of them old.

For the cultivated and assimilated Jew of any of these countries, but perhaps especially for those in Germany, who considered themselves Germans first and Jews second, who had fought with particular distinction for their country in the First World War, the shock, when it came, was a great one.

When Hitler came to power in 1933, millions of Jews were suddenly faced with a situation which threatened not only their way of life but their very existence. The Jews of Europe numbered more than 7,500,000 and, mindful of the growing crisis, many fled. One of the eminent Israelis whom I interviewed made an early decision to leave. As I was ushered into his office, I saw a short man with a broad grin come round the large desk to shake hands. Yitzhak Shamir was certainly not the terrifying figure I had been led to believe he would be. He pointed to a nearby chair and we began to discuss what had taken him to Palestine so many years before:

> I suppose it was a newsboy calling out on the corner of the street where we lived in Warsaw. It was 1933, and although of course we knew of the danger that threatened all Jews at that time, it was the shock of hearing his actual voice, and what he was calling out, that tipped the balance. It was a special edition of the paper. I went out and bought a copy, and read about how Hitler's Propaganda Minister, Dr Josef Goebbels, was planning to visit Warsaw. My immediate thought was that this was the end for Poland, and that the best thing I could do was go home and pack. So that's what I did. Soon after, I left for the Land of Israel.

Many of the Jews who arrived from Europe in the mid-1930s had already been living with anti-Semitism for some time. Hitler's seizure of power may have been the deciding factor, but for them to leave the country of their birth and head for a new land of their own was not always a wrench. For Shimon Peres, a brutal murder was the first sign that life in Poland was changing dramatically. The wide desk that separated us made it difficult to hear his soft voice as he recalled that time of his youth:

I suppose I was unaware of any sense of anti-Semitism, at least not until I reached the age of ten. At that time a terrible crime was committed in our village. One of the villagers had been found murdered in the woods. It seems that a gang of anti-Semitic thugs had murdered the man. I still remember to this day the press photographs of the body of the poor man. It was something I'll never forget. Was this the reason we left Poland? Not exactly. Part of the family, three aunts and their families, had already left for Palestine and were sending back postcards of how wonderful it was. The pictures on the front usually showed buildings – and the place looked so clean and sunny that we all felt how wonderful it must be to live there. I remember one day they sent us a crate of oranges. They were wrapped in the kind of pink paper that oranges are usually wrapped in. We all took an orange and unwrapped it and smelt it. At first we weren't interested in eating them, just in smelling them.

As a tourist from Canada, my late friend Ben Dunkelman, later to fight in Palestine, was travelling through Germany in the early 1930s. He had just settled back in a railway carriage when he was joined by an affable young German called Heinrich:

We had a pleasant chat in English, and at one point in the conversation I mentioned Hitler. "Oh, Hitler," said Heinrich. "I know little about him. He will never be important in Germany." This pleased me. Then Heinrich added as an afterthought, "But he's right about the Jews!"

I was astounded. Then Heinrich said, "After the war, 2,000,000 Jews came to Berlin, from Galicia in Poland. Now they control all the important business and industry in Berlin. Soon they will control all Germany. Hitler is right!"

I was flabbergasted. I told him that there were no more than 600,000 Jews in Germany and that most of them had lived in the country for generations. They were assimilated into German society and were more German than the Germans.

I continued to press him. He finally admitted that he did not know for sure. There were no Jews in the little Bavarian hamlet where he lived; in fact, he had never met a Jew in his life. "I'm Jewish," I told him coldly. At first he refused to believe me. Then he was terribly embarrassed. We both fell silent. There was nothing much left to say.

*

Jona Rosenfeld, whom we have met arriving in Haifa on a cruise ship, was puzzled by the Nazi parades she saw as a little girl in Germany:

> I remember vividly sitting on my balcony and watching the Brownshirts marching by, singing a song that went something like: "When Jewish blood spurts from the knife ... everything goes twice as well." Something like that. I felt bewildered. First of all, it all happened in the middle of the night. They were carrying torches and it was very dramatic; but I couldn't understand what the words of the song meant. I wondered if the blood worked as some kind of oil to make something work better. I just didn't understand.

1 April 1933 was proclaimed a boycott day by the Nazis. Jewish businesses, shops, doctors' surgeries and lawyers' chambers were to be shunned. Although Zvi Nordheimer's father had been a German soldier in the First World War, the fact that he was a Jew was all that mattered to the new masters of Germany:

> On the day of the boycott my father put on the Iron Cross, Second Class, that he had earned during the Great War, and set out to open the head office of our business, which was on Peterstrasse. In front of the shop was a young SA man, who said to my father, "Where did you steal that Iron Cross, you dirty Jew?" My father answered, "I earned it as a German soldier, fighting in the front line during the war." The Nazi replied, "That's a barefaced lie. All Jews are cowards and malingerers."
>
> At that my father turned on his heel, came home, gathered the entire family together and told us, "From this day onward we are Jews. As such, there is only one place on earth that we belong, and that is the Land of Israel. And if our enemies proclaim that we are parasites who can exist only by doing business at their expense, then we should earn a living from now on by working with our hands and becoming farmers. People such as these are needed to establish the Land of Israel."

Liddy Wohl finished school in Germany in the summer of 1933 and at almost the same time discovered to her horror that the

Nazis had already begun to introduce legislation restricting the freedom of Jewish citizens:

> I wanted to be a teacher but the university was now closed to Jews. Everything started to go downhill for us. I looked for a job, and found one in a Jewish office. My first day at work was a Saturday and on my way there I passed a number of Jewish shops. In each of the windows was a piece of yellow paper, to show that the shop was owned by a Jew. I arrived at the office and I was met by my boss, who told me that it was very nice that I had shown up but as today was a boycott day I could go home, and come back on Monday. But I'd already made up my mind that I wasn't going to stay in Germany.
>
> One day, when I was still at school, we had a visit from a member of the Jewish Agency, who told the class all about Palestine. I returned home and told my mother that I had made up my mind. I wanted to go to Palestine. I was eighteen. My mother, who was divorced, was frightened. She looked at me and said that she didn't understand what I was saying. But I was determined. I joined a Zionist youth group to prepare for the trip to Palestine. I also went to the library and read all I could about the Land of Israel. The Nazis hadn't banned such books yet. Even though I loved Germany and thought of myself as a good German, I felt that I'd seen the writing on the wall. I continued to work, and to think about Palestine. I couldn't wait to get away.
>
> When the time came for us to renew our passports, even my mother was growing uneasy about the situation in Germany. She decided then that if I was really going to go to Palestine, she and my brother would join me.

Zvi Nordheimer came from a wealthy Jewish family. He'd been attending one of Germany's best schools when he heard about a project run by the Jewish Religious Community of Leipzig and the Hechaluz – the pioneering organisation of the Zionist Workers' Movement – to provide a course in agriculture that summer. He registered for Hebrew lessons and applied for a place in the camp where the course was to be held. He wasn't yet eighteen – the minimum age requirement – but he was accepted anyway. Now he had to tell his headmaster that he was leaving – and for good:

He was greatly astonished and asked me why I was leaving and what
my future plans were. When I told him I was going into farming,
he nearly fell off his chair with surprise. But once he'd understood
what was at stake, his eyes filled with tears. He was a refined man,
a German of the old school, who had only just begun to understand
what was happening to our country.

One glimmer of light in the spreading darkness of Naziism
was the news that David Ben-Gurion had been elected Chief
Spokesman of the World Zionist Organisation. Curiously, this
was the first time that a Palestine Jew had been elected to high
office within WZO; but now this remarkable man had even
greater powers to direct the policies needed to consolidate a
true homeland for the Jewish people. The Jews of Palestine
were relieved. Ben-Gurion was exactly the kind of leader they
needed – a man with confidence in the future and a man with
the ability to convince those who were planning to make the
Aliyah that their decision was right.

Chapter Eight: A Home for Youth

As the 1930s progressed, Hitler introduced ever harsher regulations curtailing the freedom of Jewish Germans. The Nuremberg Laws, introduced towards the end of 1935, progressively took away their right to own pets or have radios, restricted their use of swimming pools, theatres, cinemas and public parks, and denied them the right to practise journalism, law and medicine freely, or to work in the arts or as teachers. More and more of them turned their thoughts to escape. The ones who had the greatest stake in the future of the Jewish race, the young, soon found themselves encouraged by their families to set their sights on Palestine. With the help of the exceptional wife of a Berlin rabbi, Recha Freier, a movement was founded under the name of Youth Aliyah. Many of today's population in Israel can say with pride that they were part of this remarkable exodus. Zvi Nordheimer joined a youth group in Germany to prepare for his new life in Israel:

> For the first time, I came into contact with Jews who were completely different from those I had known up until that point. For the most part, the young people with whom I now worked came from families of *Ostjuden* – East European Jews. From them I quickly learned Hebrew songs, and how to dance the *hora*. The hard work in the stables and in the fields didn't bother me.

However anxious they were to get to Palestine, though, most of them were still of school age, and even those who had already left school had much to learn. Their inexperience, as they learned the skills needed to become farmers, showed itself on one memorable occasion in particular, as Zvi Nordheimer remembers. They were roused in the middle of the night by their teachers:

> We were told that a cow had begun calving and that we were needed to help. We entered the pitch-dark stall and were given a rope and told to pull on one end. We had already worked up quite a sweat when somebody finally came in with a lantern, and then we saw that the rope was tied to a post. There was no cow or calf to be seen! Then we were allowed to go back to bed.

These same youths, and thousands more like them, would soon be seen with rucksacks on their backs, making their way to the agricultural villages of Palestine. Later, they would prove to be a vital force in the defence of their homeland. The settlements found them willing volunteers in learning the art of self-defence, and within weeks many of them were undergoing illegal arms training by night, learning in addition the use of Morse Code and how to break down, clean and reassemble a rifle. Alongside this training, pure experience completed their knowledge of farming.

The Jews of Poland who had the foresight to do so were joining them. As we talked, Shimon Peres took a pencil from his desk and glanced at the writing on its side as he thought back to the time that his father had left the rest of the family in Poland and headed for Palestine:

> He wrote to us frequently, telling us how wonderful things were. He had decided that the best thing for all of us would be if he left first and got settled before sending for us. Of course at this time the British Mandate was in place. The British by then had introduced regulations which required any person entering the country as an immigrant to bring a minimum of £1,000 with them – otherwise they would have to apply for an entry visa. My father had been very careful and had managed to save the amount that was needed.

Naturally, we all looked forward to his letters. Sometimes he would include photographs of himself and his business partner. Both of them looked so fit and tanned that it made us look forward all the more to the time when we could go and join them.

A large number of the Jews fleeing Europe were far from poor. Many were extremely successful businessmen in the countries of their birth. The parents of David Shenhabi lived not far from the Czechoslovak frontier:

We were an upper-middle-class family. My father, who'd always wanted to go to Palestine, left a year before the rest. Then my mother and sister followed, by which time my father had started a business. My grandparents thought we were idiots to go; but when the danger really threatened, three days before Hitler marched into Czechoslovakia, my father and some friends in Palestine chartered a Polish aeroplane, flew to Prague and got all the rest of the family out in the nick of time.

When Zvi Nordheimer's family left, they found that their chauffeur was reluctant to be parted from them:

He drove us to the station at six in the morning. There, he said goodbye to us with tears in his eyes. "Can't you take me with you?" he said. He later wrote to us that he'd felt like a dog which had lost its master.

My father, unlike other wealthy Jews, had never accumulated much in the way of significant property. He didn't own a house or land that he could sell in order to raise the money necessary for the journey and to get us settled in Israel. In fact, all his money was invested in the business he owned in partnership with his brothers. But his brothers were hard-pressed themselves, trying to realise their assets. It was a bad time for Jews. However, my father, luckily, was able to borrow all the money we needed from a good friend.

In keeping with the general atmosphere of dissolution, it was a gloomy, overcast day when three large removal vans drove up to our place. We loaded all the household goods that were destined for auction into two of them. In the third lorry was a large crate, five metres by two by two, called a "lift", in which we packed everything that we wanted to take with us to Israel. We'd taken advice about other things we might need when we got there, and we'd bought, among other things, a tiny refrigerator that ran on petrol – we'd been told that there was no electricity in Palestine.

Most journeys couldn't begin without a visit to the passport office. Liddy Wohl, trying to get out of Germany in 1933, felt that the easiest way to get round the authorities was to lie to them:

Of course we couldn't tell them that we were going to Palestine, so we said we were off to visit friends and relatives in Budapest. We left for Leipzig in December 1933, and travelled on from there to the Czech border. They stopped the train at the frontier and Nazi officials came on board to check the passports. I was terrified that they would stop us leaving, but everything was in order and we got out of Germany safely.

Bianca Romano-Segre's husband was the Secretary of the Jewish Community of Milan. He was asked to hand over a list of prominent local Jews to a Fascist organisation:

We decided not to. Instead, we sold everything we had as quickly as we could and made arrangements to go to Palestine. My husband's family had lived in Italy for centuries – since the time of the Romans; and my own family was very distressed at our departure. But we felt that we had to go. There was so much danger in the air.

We made our way to Trieste and took a ship from there. Of course we had not been able to get visas, so we had to come in illegally, as tourists.

The two Nuremberg Laws of 15 September 1935, which were signed by Hitler personally, withdrew rights of German citizenship to Jews and also forbade marriage between Jews and "German nationals". Marriages which were consecrated "in defiance" of the new law were deemed invalid, and couples already in mixed marriages were put under pressure to divorce. Jews were also forbidden to fly the German flag.

Hitler originally intended simply to drive the Jews from

German soil – there was even a plan at one stage to deport them *en masse* to Madagascar – but as his obsession and power increased, and as it became apparent that there were very few places where the Jews could go or which would accept them in unlimited numbers, so the plan of annihilation formed in his mind. This would not take formal shape until January 1942, when the "Final Solution" was planned at a villa in Wannsee, a suburb of Berlin; but concentration camps for political detainees were being set up in Germany by the summer of 1933 and mass executions were taking place behind the German front line in Poland almost as soon as that country had been conquered. On the level of day-to-day life, most Jewish Germans, who had lived peacefully with their Gentile neighbours for years, suddenly found after Hitler's seizure of power that they were no longer wanted – they were rejected and hated.

The Palestine Jewish community viewed Hitler's arrival with alarm. Ben-Gurion, in the face of a generally indifferent world, immediately began to make plans to open the gates of Palestine as widely as possible to all the persecuted Jews who wished to come there.

At first, the German government was happy to allow the Jews to go, though stripped of most of their property and money; since Palestine was willing to take responsibility, the solution seemed simple. However, the Americans did not increase their immigration quota, agreed in 1924, of 25,957 per year (in fact the total entry figure for 1934-35 was only 5,201) and the British Government's Palestine White Paper of 17 May 1939 restricted the number of Jews allowed into that country to a maximum of 15,000 per year over the next five years, with no promise of an increase after that – rather the opposite. The White Paper largely met the latest Arab demands and evoked a furious and bitter response from the Jewish Agency for Palestine.

In fact, the British authorities in Palestine allowed in more Jews in 1939 than in the whole of the previous two years – about 27,500, which brought the total immigration of Jews since 1936 to about 80,000; but few British officials in London had great sympathy for the Jews, and the quota was suspended completely for the six-month period between October 1939 and March 1940.

The Jews of central Europe were looking increasingly trapped. But those who could make it were determined to suffer the journey, however wearing the route may have been. The German parents of Yehuda Ariel knew Palestine already, having been there on their honeymoon in 1913. They returned there to live in 1935:

They'd wanted to leave in 1929, and they would have done, too, if it hadn't been for the terrible riots that took place in Palestine then. There were six of us small children, so my parents put off going. When I was a bit older I left school and went to do a course in agriculture sponsored by a Zionist group. Then, in 1935, we left Frankfurt. First, we took a train to Trieste – that took the whole night. In Trieste we boarded a ship called the *Jerusalem*.

Most of the passengers were new immigrants who had come from all over Europe – from Poland and Hungary mostly. The voyage took five or six days, and the night before we arrived we couldn't sleep for excitement. We stood on the deck, waiting for our first sight of the Holy Land. When we finally saw the coast we burst into tears, and then started singing in our joy.

Chapter Nine: Arrival

The ports of Haifa and Jaffa welcomed most of the immigrants. But they were ill-equipped for the task, having no deep water close enough to land to receive the large ships which carried most of the newcomers, who were therefore ferried ashore in small boats. It wasn't always easy to clamber down Jacob's ladders from the ocean-going ship that had brought you, into the perilously bobbing rowing boats moored alongside which were waiting to take you to land.

Along with the immigrants came cargoes of all kinds – merchandise and raw materials for Palestine. The ports were bustling and colourful, and made a vivid impression on the new arrivals. Shimon Peres had travelled to Istanbul by train, and from there took a Polish ship to Jaffa. I asked him if he remembered his arrival:

Vividly. No one who arrived in Palestine at that time will ever forget the scenes in the ports. Crowds of merchants in small boats swarmed around our ship, selling all manner of things: drinks, orange juice, even palm branches. The oarsmen wore colourful clothes. Some had wide pantaloons on, and turbans on their heads. These same boats would ferry you ashore for a small fee, and most of the passengers had no choice but to take them. We were lucky; my father was there to meet us in a small boat of his own. He bustled us aboard, and the moment we reached the shore he steered us adroitly through customs, so we had a relatively easy time of it.

After taking the train from Germany to Trieste with his brother, Mr Justice Hirim Cohen, as he now is, found a Palestine-bound ship:

> My father was very rich, so my brother and I were able to travel first class. The passage was fine, but when we arrived at Jaffa we found we were in for a shock. Boatmen came out to take us to the shore, but the swell was so big that we could not go down the Jacob's ladders. The sailors on board simply picked us up and threw us from the deck down into the little boats below! That was fine for us, since we were healthy young men; but old people got just the same treatment.

Rita Bresler, from Germany, was five years old when her father decided that enough was enough. If he could get a certificate, the family would emigrate:

> He did, and we left. We sailed to Palestine from Italy. I remember that they served tomato soup on the ship – I hated it! I hate it to this day! But I made friends with another little girl on board and that friendship has lasted ever since.
>
> Before we got to Jaffa, someone on the ship told me that we'd be taken ashore from the ship by men wearing baggy pants, and that if I didn't behave, the men would put me in their pants and hide me there. It was a stupid joke. I was lowered into the arms of a perfectly nice Arab boatman, but he was wearing pantaloons and of course I was terrified. As a matter of fact, it's still a haunting memory.

As we have seen, it was a distinct advantage to have relatives or friends already in Palestine when you arrived. All the newcomers needed time to adjust and acclimatise, and in such circumstances familiar faces helped. Sam Bresler had friends from Austria who introduced him to a kibbutz:

> It had been started by a group of middle-class Germans and it was isolated, so it was a little bit dangerous. The Germans needed a bunch

of physically tougher people than they were to do the spadework, so we set to as hired labourers. It was a hard life, but it became even harder when some of us contracted typhus. Soon it had spread to everyone. Anyone with typhus was sent to a government isolation hospital, because it was so infectious. I got to know the hospital well.

For Yehuda Ariel, the feeling of arrival was wonderful, and any nostalgia he felt for his old homeland quickly dissolved:

We felt at home immediately. We had cut off all and any connection with Germany. We didn't even want to speak German!

As soon as we could, we went to see the Wailing Wall and all the other holy places – it was something we'd been looking forward to doing for so long. Jerusalem! Even so, it was a far cry from what we'd been expecting. The paupers that clustered around the Wailing Wall, begging, were so pathetic that it's hard to describe them. And people lived really simply. They couldn't even afford to travel by bus, and they used to walk miles and miles, everywhere. Even the ones who were a bit better off still didn't go in for much luxury.

As we had relatives and friends already in Jerusalem, we didn't feel at all lonely. In fact we lived with some of our friends until my parents had found a flat in Tel Aviv. By that time our container had arrived from Germany with all the furniture which my parents had ordered specially for Israel: not the old, heavy stuff, but modern, light tables and chairs.

I started work straight away. First of all I helped my father to set up his business and then I went to Mikve Israël, an agricultural vocational high school which also trained its students to get acclimatised to life in Palestine. After that, I wandered from one place to another, working in the farms and in the fields of the settlers who were already established. We had very primitive implements. In fact, we did nearly everything by hand – just like in the Middle Ages.

Then I worked in the orange groves, alongside the Arab labourers, and later on I drove tractors and combine-harvesters; so I can honestly say that I tried everything. As the farm jobs were seasonal, I worked out-of-season in the construction industry, even once as a hod-carrier! I used to wander from one place to another with a rucksack on my back and a suitcase in my hand, asking for work.

We'd brought a wireless with us from Germany, so we were able to follow the European news: we knew all about what was happening, and we heard more from the refugees who came after us. My grandmother lived in the Netherlands, where my mother came from. She was an old woman. My mother used to visit her every couple of years. The last time she went was in 1937. We never saw my grandmother again, or any of my mother's other Dutch relatives. They all perished in the Holocaust.

Not everyone arrived by ship. Liddy Wohl, travelling with her brother, her mother and a friend, came overland, and was glad that they had brought so few belongings with them as they crossed the frontier from Turkey into Syria:

All of us had to carry our suitcases, and some people were carrying lots of belongings. I remember one woman who was wearing a number of dresses, one over another, to save carrying them. It was February and we were on a mountain pass. It was very cold.

The Syrians were waiting for us at the border. They spoke Arabic and French, so I had to use my school French to talk to them. They took us to a little mountain refuge. There, they sent the men to the stable to sleep, and allowed us to use the bunks in the cabin.

I don't think they knew we were Jewish. They didn't ask for our passports, and the next morning they put us all into taxis. I thought we were being taken to a hotel, but we arrived at a police station. We told the police we were on our way to Iraq, but when they searched our luggage they found a letter my boss had given me in Germany, introducing me to a friend of his in Palestine. I told the policeman it wasn't mine, that it was a letter I'd promised to post for someone, but forgotten. He didn't insist.

After what seemed an age more travelling, we arrived in Beirut, where we stayed for a month in a very primitive inn, sleeping on the floor. One evening we were told to be ready to leave at midnight the following day, but we wouldn't be able to take all our luggage with us. In the morning my friend and I went down to the docks and saw there a luxury liner which was on a cruise of the Mediterranean. The passengers were disembarking for a day's sightseeing. We went up to a Jewish-looking couple, explained our predicament and asked if they would take our suitcases to Tel Aviv for us. By luck, that is where they came from, and they were really nice and agreed to help us. They gave us their address and told us we could pick up our luggage when we arrived.

That night, we waited for the two small buses which were to pick us up, but they didn't arrive until 1.30 a.m. Then one left, but ours remained where it was. I have always been an impatient person, so it wasn't long before I asked the driver why we were waiting. He told me to mind my own business. Then, suddenly, an Arab woman dressed in black appeared. She and her husband, who was with her, were also going to Palestine illegally. They'd just got married.

At last the bus got moving and we drove and drove and drove. Finally at about 4 a.m. it stopped and the guide who was with us told us that we had to get off the bus as fast as we could and run for it. We jumped down on to sand dunes, which were very difficult to walk on, let alone run. The early-morning dew had made everything damp, but we struggled on until we came to the shore, where the people who'd been on the first bus were waiting for us. We were told to sit down and wait too. We had no idea what we were waiting for.

At about 5.30 in the morning we suddenly saw a little boat approaching. It was a fishing boat with two Arabs on board. Our guide took the first group and told them to get into the boat, but they had to wade through the icy April seawater to reach it. The boat was too small for all twenty of us, so ten of us had to wait half an hour longer for a second one to fetch us.

The boat trip had to be paid for, and it wasn't cheap, because the boatmen were engaged in dangerous work. When they came to collect us, my mother refused to go into the water. Even though she had got this far, she felt that getting her feet wet would be unladylike. Or maybe she was worried about her fur coat. Anyway, we had to carry her to the boat. As we set off, we were all told to be very quiet. There didn't seem to be anybody around, either on land or sea, but us, but we did as we were told. It was very still, and eerie. We were crushed together and one girl was seasick, but we were in a good mood because we had nearly reached our goal. Once well out of sight of land we were able to sing, and we did, happily, though we had practically no food all day and going to the lavatory presented a problem: we just had to turn our backs to give the one who was doing it a bit of privacy.

Before we got near the shore we could see the calmer water, and the first sight of Haifa was very exciting. We all had to lie down in the bottom of the boat and keep very still as we made our way inshore; there were searchlights playing the harbour, looking for illegal immigrants: plenty of us were trying to come in and the British weren't very happy with that. It had to look as if only the two Arab boatmen were aboard. It was 7.30 in the evening when we arrived, and we were very excited. We headed south, hugging the shore in the dark, until suddenly we saw a little headland, where we rendezvoused with the other boat.

When we were pretty close to land, our guide told us to jump into the water. The water was quite deep, but we were able to carry my mother ashore and I managed to keep the little case I had kept with me dry. The moment our feet touched land, the boats turned about and were gone.

Now we were alone on the beach. My mother was kissing the ground. I don't know whether it was because she had finally reached the Promised Land or because she was pleased to be on any land at all after the boat! We looked around, and there was no one else to be seen. Everyone was wet and cold. The guide seemed to have disappeared. I thought we were lost. Like a sheep, I began to follow those walking ahead of us. There was no moon and it was very dark. Then we heard a noise and saw two huge lamps, like eyes, coming towards us. A train. We located the track and followed it until we came to a road. It was the road to Haifa, though I didn't know that then. But we were lucky. It turned out that two of the men with us knew the area already, and I now realised that we'd been following them. The guide had gone on ahead to get help and met us with a bus – so in fact everything had been well thought out.

The bus was parked a good way off the road with its lights off. They called out our names in the dark, and one by one we climbed aboard. I became impatient again. When I saw a car on the road some way off, I thought I'd go and hail it and get a lift, rather than wait for the bus to get going, but it had passed long before I could reach the road. Luckily for me. When I was on the bus I told the guide what I'd planned to do and he was furious. He said, "It was lucky for all of us that it didn't stop. It was a police car."

When we arrived in Haifa the group was split up, and we were sent to different private houses. The main reason for this was to make it as hard as possible for the authorities to locate us, if they got wind of an illegal landing. The people at the house we were sent to were very kind. They gave us something to eat and, even more importantly, dry clothes. My mother, of course, wasn't wet. I borrowed her fur coat to keep warm. Then, after we'd eaten, we all slept in one double bed – Mother, my friend, my brother and I.

The next day we made our way to the centre of Haifa where I bought a new pair of shoes – the ones I'd had had given out towards the end of our journey. We stayed two weeks longer in Haifa, and then made our way to Tel Aviv, where my suitcase was waiting for me.

Liddy found work as a carpenter, which seems not without irony, given where she was:

I made doors. The place I worked in was huge and every morning when we arrived the rats and mice scattered. They brought the water we needed on the backs of donkeys. I lasted for a year, but then the men went on strike because I did the same work as they did for less money, and the boss liked me for that.

When his ship dropped anchor just outside the port of Jaffa, the family of Zvi Nordheimer remained on board and continued on to Haifa:

We were lodged initially at the Immigrant Shelter at Mount Carmel, which at that time was located on a hill far outside the town, in lonely and desolate surroundings. The shelter itself was uncomfortable, cold and austere, because it was still in the process of being built, and only the shell of the building, with bare, unplastered concrete walls, was complete. The wind whistled through the holes where the windows should have been.

We met a young woman in a shop who had also arrived from Germany and who seemed quite cheerful and contented. We struck up a conversation with her, and she told us that she and her husband, like many young couples, had found places at the Agricultural Co-operative of Nahalal in the Jezreel Valley. When we went there to see the mayor of the settlement, we found him lying on the floor of his wooden hut, reading the newspaper. It was the hour of his midday rest, he explained to us, and it was coolest on the floor.

The welcome that Justice Hirim Cohen received was a little too much:

> People on shore – even at the customs – were so generous with their gifts of biscuits and cakes that I was sick all day afterwards because I had eaten too much! As soon as I felt better we set out for Jerusalem. The bus that took us there was really more of a flat-top lorry. There were planks along each side to stop people from falling off the sides. The journey took from seven in the morning until three in the afternoon. To say that it was uncomfortable is an understatement, but even though there were no forests at that time and the countryside was brown, I found both the landscape and the people beautiful.
>
> When we arrived in Jerusalem the first thing we did was start looking for a room. As a stop-gap, we took a place sharing with another family and without a lavatory. We didn't stay long, and soon afterwards we had the luck to be able to rent a room in one of the most elegant houses in Jerusalem. Of course, the most important thing about it was that it had a bathroom attached to it – a really smart one. The beauty of this was that we could share it with our friends, since most of them lived in very sorry circumstances, and nobody else had a bathroom.

Rita Bresler found attitudes in great contrast to those in Europe:

> The strangest thing about society was that money was unimportant. Achievement, at school or at work – that was the most important thing. The prominent members of society when I was growing up did not owe their position to wealth, but to what they had done.

She also remembers intimate details of those early days:

> My father used to take me to the museum in Tel Aviv when I was a little girl. That was always our big day out. My father loved art, and we watched the museum grow from the three-roomed flat where it started. Another thing I still think about sometimes is Dr Shortstein's pet shop. There were puppies and kittens in the window, and there was a parrot he used to sing to.

An area called Rehovot, just south of Tel Aviv, was Shimon Peres' first home:

> It's difficult to describe. It was a large village. There were no pavements, and our playground was the orchards. The best thing of all was that the weather was so good, we could dress in our summer clothes all the time. No more shirts and ties and suits, just casual clothes – short-sleeved shirts and khaki trousers.

I had heard that one of the first jobs Peres found was an unusual one. He laughed as he explained:

> That's true. It was certainly different. I worked as a shepherd. Looking back, I can see that, like most jobs, it gave me an opportunity to learn. For one thing I had my first lesson in how to get along with others. In this case, the cows and the lambs. The other advantage of the job was that it gave me the perfect opportunity to practise my pistol-shooting. I'd get up in the mornings at about four and practise firing when no one was around except the cows and the lambs, who soon got used to it. But they didn't get used to the flies. As soon as the sun came up the flies would arrive and begin biting the cows. It drove them crazy and they would scatter everywhere, making it very difficult for me to round them up again.

When David Shenhabi's family landed in Jaffa,

> We didn't bring a lot of luggage – only those things we really needed. Father had written us letters describing what we would see. I stayed with my parents for three days while they moved into a flat, but then I decided to join a kibbutz. My father wasted no time in getting settled, and immediately set himself up in work by starting the first dry-cleaning business in Palestine. As there was no sewer in Tel Aviv yet, he built the plant in Jaffa; unfortunately it was completely destroyed in the Arab riots of 1936. It was a big setback for him, but he soon rallied. As he was a trained engineer, he managed to get work with the British, working for the Post Office.

The group that David himself linked up with decided that they would found a new kibbutz:

The Jewish Agency gave us some land in the Jordan Valley. There was a great deal of discussion; not everyone liked the idea of starting a kibbutz there because it was on the Syrian border and it was surrounded by Arab villages. In order to defend the camp, I was sent on all sorts of courses, which lasted between one and three months; and all this training had to be done in secret. Then one day I heard that a kibbutz had been started on the border with Lebanon, and that they were asking for volunteers to help celebrate the opening and to stay for a month. A friend of mine volunteered and got killed by a sniper the first night. The next day they asked for a replacement and I volunteered. I was there for three months. Our average age was about twenty-three, and there were both men and women there.

In the beginning experts from other kibbutzim who had more experience would come and give us talks, teach us about bricklaying and things like that. The work was hard because we had to construct buildings and develop the land for farming. In the evenings we'd take a shower, have dinner and then have a dance or hold a meeting. On Fridays we always danced until late at night because we rested on the Sabbath. There were about fifty of us, and everything we did was decided democratically.

Despite the increased restrictions on their official entry into Palestine, the pressure on those fleeing the Nazi scourge was too great for them not to take the risk of getting to the new Jewish homeland and entering it by whatever means possible. The Jews of Europe knew that their old way of life had gone forever, and that the only means of survival lay in escape.

Chapter Ten: Growing Numbers

In the midst of the increasing violence in Palestine, the numbers of refugees arriving in the country continued to grow. Nothing the British or the Arabs could do stopped the ingress of Jews who fled Europe in the 1930s. Many thousands arrived from Germany, bringing with them not only capital, at least in the early days before the new anti-Semitic Nazi laws took hold, but, even more importantly, expertise in a wide range of fields, from medicine to the arts, from the sciences to scholarship. They were also workers, and they pioneered new settlements in the stony countryside of Judea.

Professor Peter Gradenwitz was born in Berlin, where he studied music. He was just about to start a new course of study, in philosophy, at Freiburg, when he was told that, as a Jew, he was excluded from German universities. But he had met and fallen in love with the daughter of a friend, and through her he learned about Palestine. Before long, he became convinced that Palestine was the place they should go. They married and then made their way to London. From there they ultimately set off for the Holy Land, following a tortuous route via Holland and Trieste where, like so many others, they took ship:

I had a job with the piano factory in Tel Aviv waiting for me, since that was the work I had done in London. About a week after we arrived we managed to find a flat. The evening after we'd moved in we decided to take a stroll around our new neighbourhood. As we closed the front door of the flat behind us, one of our new neighbours said, "Why close it? You need air, leave it open." So we did.

Soon after we'd arrived the Arab riots started; but despite them we were all very excited about the possibility of Toscanini coming to conduct a concert. Nobody believed it was really going to happen, so subscriptions were very few. Then suddenly in mid-December it was confirmed. Toscanini was on his way to Palestine. All the subscriptions were snapped up within days!

The largest numbers of Jewish immigrants came from Eastern Europe. These people had clung to their faith through decades of prejudice and now found themselves wedged between Hitler on one side and Stalin on the other. However, many of them were convinced socialists. Shimon Peres, who has himself written on the subject, told me of his own later experience:

The first thing you must understand is that the students at the high school I attended in Israel were for the most part pretty wealthy. I was not. Like many young people, of that time and now, I was trying to find a niche for myself. One of the easiest ways of doing that was to find the youth movement which best reflected your own beliefs at the time. I joined a Labour Union, and that action set me apart from my fellow students. In fact, I was the only Labour supporter in the whole school.

There was another school near the border, at a place called Ben Shimon. I had a friend who was already at this school, so when my instructor in the youth movement asked me if I'd like to join him, I said yes. Like many others at the time the school was based on an agricultural kibbutz, and most of the students there were ardent socialists. Some of them felt very strongly that we should follow the Russian model. You must understand that much of Jewish literature is steeped in socialism, and that many Jews lean to the left. Marx himself was a Jew, and those immigrants from the USSR at the time did see Marxism as the correct political path for Israel to follow. I disagreed with this, and although I'd certainly studied Marx, I think my main reason for doing so was to impress my wife!

The countryside was dotted with Arab villages, with kibbutzim springing up among them, but the towns were changing rapidly, teeming with people of all colours and cultures. Trying their best to maintain their role as the governing force within this melting-pot were the British. One shock for the newly arrived immigrants was the sheer number of British soldiers. I asked Peres about this:

> Oh yes, they were everywhere, but one got used to them. The officers looked quite impressive, with their polished belts and their swaggersticks. They'd stand around, slapping their sticks against their thighs, and I can't say that we were all that fond of them, since we were sure that they sided with the Arabs. The Bedouin are an easy people to like; they're very generous and they are famous for their hospitality. They were certainly better at making friends with the British than we were.

But by no means all the British soldiers took the Arab side. Orde Charles Wingate, who was later to lead the Chindits in Burma and die fighting the Japanese in 1944, saw service in Palestine and Transjordan in the late 1930s. He felt so strongly that the Jews had a right to defend themselves that he began to train volunteers in the art of guerrilla warfare. Each night he would make his way into the hills to rendezvous with his "troops", whom he quickly formed into a Haganah squad of night fighters. Known as Wingate's Raiders, their main purpose was to break up Arab gangs bent on attacking the settlements; but unfortunately their actions weren't sufficient to put a stop to Arab harassment. Tension continued to grow, and it was clear that the Mandate could not function for much longer unless something was done.

David Ben-Gurion was a strong leader, but there were those in Palestine who felt that he wasn't tough enough. They believed that if the Arabs continued to attack the settlements and cause widespread havoc, the only answer was to fight fire with fire. And not only would the Arabs be targeted; the British would be as well. Both the Irgun and a new militant organisation, the Fighters for the Freedom of Israel (known to the British as the Stern Gang, after its leader, a young poet called Avraham Stern)

concentrated on forcing the British to leave Palestine through a
programme of terror. Government offices and police stations
became their main targets.

Binyamin Gonen was at secondary school when a girl who
was already a member of the Stern Gang interested him in
joining. Everyone he confided in was against it, and they were
in good company. Ben-Gurion was furious at the terrorism. He
believed that the Jews, the Arabs and the British could find a
way to live together peacefully through negotiations. To back
his claim, he reminded all those who would listen that Britain
had, after all, allowed 350,000 Jews to settle in Palestine, had
built the port of Haifa and been responsible for the road network
upon which nascent Jewish industry depended. And, not content
with showing the British that he favoured a peaceful means of
settlement, he delivered the same message to the Arab leaders.
It was hard to dispute the sense of what he said: Arab village
and Jewish settlement existed cheek by jowl, and on a local level
Jews and Arabs would come together from time to time in the
realisation that through co-operation everyone would benefit.
Zvi Nordheimer found this out very quickly:

We certainly didn't want to fight the Arabs. Fighting the land was
bad enough. I remember that moles inflicted great devastation on
vegetable crops. They ate the roots and destroyed entire fields. They
also carried potatoes back to their burrows, storing them for the
winter. An acquaintance of ours invented and built a device that a
tunnelling mole triggered automatically when it pushed at the dirt.
In a manner of speaking, the mole would shoot itself.

Early on, we had a lot of contact with local Arab merchants, most
of whom lived in the nearby village of Tamra. They kept us supplied
with sheep manure, straw bedding, barley for the horses and carob
for the cows, all of which they delivered in large sacks, carried on
the backs of camels.

Our main supplier was a slim, handsome man called Fadil, who
always brought his young son along. They often stayed for breakfast
and, as we'd picked up some Arabic, we could communicate after a
fashion.

But as soon as serious trouble broke out across the country between
Arab and Jew, we lost contact with them. Later on, when things had

been patched up, one of Fadil's brothers told us that he had suddenly fallen ill and died. With his last breath, Fadil had called his son to him and told him to visit us and re-establish the contact between our families as soon as it was possible to do so, regardless of whether we did business with one another. Fadil described us as his best friends. And indeed, the son did come and see us.

David Bar-Illan's father worked for the Iraq Petroleum Company, which had more Arab employees than Jews, and yet there was no bigotry: everyone regarded everyone else as a friend and colleague, and the unrest in the country did nothing to disturb this state of affairs.

Harmony was possible and did occur. Despite the Mufti's intractable position, Ben-Gurion continued to strive for it, arranging meetings with Arab landowners to reassure them that he understood their concerns and to tell them that if they would only sit down and discuss their mutual problems with the Jews, both sides could work together for the common good of the country. However, he was rebuffed by the Arab Higher Committee, who remained adamant that the Jews should vacate all land deemed by the Committee to be historically Arab. If they would not, the Arabs would make life impossible for them. The Committee did not let things rest there. Funded by the Italian Fascist Party, they organised a group of 5,000 guerrillas who began to make systematic attacks on Jewish settlements, even killing Arabs who were known to have Jewish sympathies.

By this point the British had acknowledged that the Jews had to have some means of self-defence within their own control; apart from anything else, the British forces in Palestine were insufficient to keep the peace, and there was neither the will nor the money at home to increase them. The Jews responded with the Haganah, already a force to be reckoned with as we have seen, but without military stores or even uniforms. Nevertheless it was an efficient defence force, and it remained true to that appellation – never striking the first blow, but responding hard and fast to aggression.

Shimon Peres joined the Haganah after only a short time in Palestine. He didn't know at the time that by doing so he would meet his partner for life:

Most of the young people in the kibbutz were being sworn into the
Haganah, and so was I. Soon after I'd been recruited, they decided
to put me in charge of a defensive position nearby. We worked the
land during the day and stood guard at night. It so happened that
the position was close to the home of a beautiful young girl, whom I
soon got to know, and in the course of time she became my wife. Her
brother was an instructor in the Haganah. Between him and her, I
learnt a lot!

The strengthening of the Haganah came none too soon; and if
the British showed no sign of altering their stance on restricted
immigration, then the Jews of Palestine covertly encouraged
those wishing to do so to make the Aliyah anyway. If there
were not enough jobs, they argued, there was certainly enough
land, even though much of it was in remote and dangerous areas.
Both the land and the people who farmed it could be defended.
Existing settlements were fortified: in the years between 1936
and 1938, thirty-six of them were surrounded with stockades
equipped with 35-foot searchlight towers.

Meanwhile the work of developing the farms and finding
means of distributing their produce continued. Zvi Nordheimer
remembers:

We soon learnt that marketing our products through a middleman
meant that he made most of the profit. This made us cultivate crops
which we could sell directly, such as strawberries and asparagus. My
father filled two large baskets with beans and spinach, and sold them
door-to-door in Qiryat Bialik. The local housewives wanted other
vegetables as well, so my father bought a little donkey cart and
bought up assorted vegetables from our fellow settlers, thus ensuring
that own our produce sold with the maximum profit,.and making an
extra small supplementary income by selling that of his friends.

It was not uncommon to find new arrivals running into acquaint-
ances they had known in their native land. Nordheimer's father
had been a rich man back home in Leipzig:

One day, while making his rounds, he met up with a man who'd been
one of his customers in Leipzig. The man could hardly believe his eyes.

He said to my father, "What! You, the wealthy Herr Nordheimer, are peddling vegetables door to door?" My father replied, "But nothing in the least has changed. My business manager in Leipzig was an ass, and so is the one I have now!"

The business spread to the Arab community, and even to the British:

The soldiers had things to sell as well. Once, when I was busy making hay out in the fields, a military vehicle drove up and came to a halt near one of the haystacks. Four soldiers jumped out. Two of them opened the bonnet and pretended to work on the engine while the others unloaded rubber boots, trousers, shirts, woollen socks and all sorts of other things which they shoved beneath the hay. "Do you want to buy these?" they asked. Of course, the stuff had all been stolen; but they sold it dirt cheap and became our suppliers of inexpensive work clothes.

Ben-Gurion was a familiar figure in the countryside, driving from place to place to talk to the settlers and the kibbutzniks who formed the backbone of the new society. One day early in his career he saw a young man hitching a lift by the roadside and told his driver to stop for him. The young man was Shimon Peres:

I was about sixteen at the time. Ben-Gurion wasn't as well known then as he later became, but I knew about his work and admired him for it. It was a thrill to ride with him, but I was grateful for more mundane reasons too – it was a cold, wintry day. I settled myself in the car and looked expectantly at Ben-Gurion, hoping to get into some sort of conversation; but he paid no attention to me. In fact, he turned his back on me and went to sleep. But after a while he woke up abruptly and asked me, out of the blue, "What do you think the best policy would be: to go to war and take the risk, or negotiate for peace and pay the price?" Perhaps luckily he didn't give me a chance to reply, but went on to talk at length about Lenin. He said that Lenin, though Trotsky's intellectual inferior, became leader because he was decisive. That was the first of many things I learned from him.

As the Second World War approached, Ben-Gurion became more and more preoccupied with ways and means of getting Jewish refugees from Europe into Palestine despite the British restrictions. He instructed the Haganah leadership both to devise plans and to organise arms purchases from wherever they could get them. The World Zionist Organisation was quick to make funds available for both ventures, and Haganah agents across the world began to mobilise.

The most obvious way to get people into Palestine was by sea, but big ships were risky, because they were too easy for the British fleet which patrolled the Mediterranean to spot. It was necessary therefore to find, equip and organise a large number of small vessels, from fishing boats to sea-going barges, no matter how dilapidated, as long as they were seaworthy. This the Haganah and its agents managed to do, with the help of the WZO funds. Prospective illegal immigrants may have baulked slightly, as they arrived at the shore, at the sight of the craft that were to carry them, but the danger at their backs spurred them forward. Some were so desperate that they would have been prepared to swim to Palestine if the need had arisen.

But the refugees were never alone. Always at their side there were members of the Haganah, directing embarkation and disembarkation, guiding, calming and encouraging. Landings in Palestine were always made at night, and there was always a welcoming group on hand for each bunch of bedraggled and bewildered newcomers. Once ashore, they found that provision had already been made to ensure their speedy assimilation into Palestine Jewish society. In advance of their arrival, their new neighbours-to-be would rapidly erect a wooden stockade around their designated dwelling-place, complete with a water tower which would double as a watch tower. By the time they had been in the country for twenty-four hours, the immigrants were the owners and occupiers of a new "village".

Although the cities, too, were attracting newcomers, it was hardly practical to increase their size and by so doing ignore those areas of the countryside which were barren and in need of cultivation. Living in such areas was never easy, as we have seen. Quite apart from the danger of isolation and the risk of attack, there was the work itself, which was simply backbreaking. Zvi Nordheimer remembers working on a new well:

> The well was being dug in Nahalal, using the completely primitive methods common at the time, in which the work was done by hand and using a device dating back almost to the beginning of human history. It consisted of a large wooden beam, balanced with a heavy weight fixed to one end, which was repeatedly raised and lowered so that it gradually bore into the ground. It was operated by a crosspiece at the opposite end of the beam to the weight. Five men worked on the crosspiece, raising and lowering the beam rhythmically for eight hours a day in the blazing heat.

There were other problems to be solved. How did one defend an outpost miles from help? Although it was considered an extremely dangerous area to be, David Bar-Illan decided to build a house on Mount Carmel; and he did so at the height of the unrest of 1938:

> Naturally, we prepared ourselves for any sign of danger. We learnt how to use guns, and we got ourselves a guard dog.
>
> There was no road to the house, just a foot-path, so it was almost impossible to reach by car. In winter, the path would get flooded and become extremely muddy. In the end, we paved it and made it into a proper road and, since it was our road and we could call it what we liked, we named it after my sister. It's still there.
>
> The closest town was a mile away. It was fascinating to live that way, but it was always fraught with danger. You had to be courageous, but so many people faced similar perils. Ours was very barren land and very few Arabs lived nearby; but those who did were not always friendly.
>
> The other thing to remember is that most of us settlers came from highly industrialised countries and when we got here we had to start from scratch. Most of the Jewish people from Europe, which is also where most of the early settlers came from, had no background in anything but urban professions and businesses which were totally useless in this country at that time. They had to learn about agriculture, and that in itself was a pioneering act. People from ghettos and *shtetls* knew virtually nothing of value in terms of modern life; and there

were very few people with experience of farming or working on the land among us.

By contrast to Bar-Illan's ascetic existence, his mother opened the first ready-to-wear dress shop in Haifa. He remembers urban life at the time:

> My childhood was marked by the first Intifada – the riots of 1936–39. During those three years my mother wasn't able to go to work at her shop, which was on Haifa's main street, without the risk of being shot at by Arab rioters. One person was gunned down right in front of her shop. Cars would be hijacked in the middle of the street, people were opening fire at random – that's how it was in those days, and over the period, something like 650 people were killed. Don't forget that the Jewish population then was still quite small, so 650 people was a large number and it was difficult to find anyone who hadn't lost someone – be it relative or friend – as a result of the Arab atrocities.
>
> But it wasn't as simple as that. Ninety per cent of my mother's customers were Arabs, and in general the relationship between the two communities in Haifa was excellent. The rioters and the killers had either been incited to make trouble, which was usually the case, or they were made up of organised gangs set up by foreign powers – it was Syria in the beginning, though later Egypt took a hand. The point is that most of the trouble was deliberately sparked by outside forces whose sole objective was to foment trouble within the community in order to destabilise it. It is very important to remember the peaceful relations we had with the Arab community. Even my father's doctor was an Arab.

The year 1936 was one that the Jews were happy to see come to an end. Meanwhile, the British made another effort to reconcile the two sides they governed so uneasily. A Royal Commission was set up under Lord Peel in the wake of the 1936 disturbances. Assisting Peel was a former Ambassador to Berlin, Sir Horace Rumbold. Peel's own background was in the Indian administration, where he had been Secretary of State, and the other members of the Commission had been selected to reflect their strict impartiality.

The Commission arrived in Palestine on the anniversary of Armistice Day, 11 November, just in time to attend a ceremony at the British Military Cemetery. Its members stayed at the King David Hotel in Jerusalem and held session at the nearby Palace Hotel. The Arab leadership refused to co-operate with the Commission, however, and daily outbursts of violence reminded Peel and his colleagues that the quest for a peaceful solution was going to be very far from easy. On 22 November, there was a momentary glimmer of hope when Emir Abdullah arrived in the city to try to persuade the Mufti to meet the Commission after all; but the Emir's attempt was in vain.

In the meantime, however, the Commission had sent one of its members south to the Negev Desert to interview someone who *was* willing to talk – Chaim Weizmann.

Chapter Eleven: Outside Advice

The blazing sun of the desert made its way towards the western horizon. In the distance, a car kicked sand into a billowing cloud as it travelled to the edge of the Negev. The Peel Commissioner inside sat next to the driver and looked out across the barren land, wondering why anyone would feel that this expanse of emptiness was worth fighting for. Yet both Jews and Arabs had made it clear that, if need be, they would fight to the last to control whatever area of sand they each felt was rightfully theirs. The problem of controlling the number of incoming Jews to the satisfaction of the Arabs had still not been resolved after years of effort, and the Jews would not accept any limitation at all.

The Commissioner was, however, convinced that a peaceful solution was still possible; and there were certainly people on both sides of the divide who were willing to work towards it. The most obvious man on the Jewish side was Chaim Weizmann, the eminent organic chemist who now spent most of his time at the Sieff Institute of Science at Rehovot. From what the Commissioner had heard, here was a man who would listen to reason; and he was hopeful that his journey to the edge of the desert would not be wasted.

At last, the car drew to a halt. The driver pointed to a series of buildings set among the dry hills which stretched south over the stony wilderness that linked Sinai to the Red Sea.

The Commissioner found Weizmann alone in his laboratory, working late by the light of a single bulb which threw a circle of light on to a small table. The Commissioner asked him what he was working on and he replied, smilingly, that he was making "an absorptive capacity".

In scientific language, Weizmann had described the problem as he saw it. He believed that the national home was in the nature of an experiment. In his eyes, the nation had to evolve organically. If the experiment were successful, the result would be an independent state.

But, as with many experiments, the result could not be predicted with absolute accuracy. Clearly, the small country the Jews hoped to have as their own could not accommodate all the world's 17 million Jews, but Weizmann felt that 3 to 4 million could live comfortably there.

This would mean a radical increase on the numbers in the 1920s. Then, Jewish immigration seldom rose above 5,000 a year. But, Weizmann explained as he sat down with the Commissioner to discuss the various problems that confronted them, a nation that had no roots in the soil on which it lived was not the answer either. Jews and Arabs alike must adapt to the environment they occupied. And contributions to the country should be made by them.

This thinking was nothing new. Back in the 1920s, Winston Churchill had accepted a tender from a Menshevik refugee named Pinchas Rutenberg to build a power station on the River Auja. This power station, close to Jaffa, supplied all Palestine with electricity. The building in which Weizmann and the Commissioner now sat had been built in 1932 because Weizmann had persuaded his friend Israel Sieff to create a scientific institute at Rehovot as a memorial to his dead son, Daniel.

As the evening progressed, the Commissioner began to feel that his trip had been worthwhile. The man sitting opposite him was more than a scientist. He was a man with a vision, able to conceive of a path to peaceful co-existence through scientific exploitation of the land. The absorptive capacity of which he had spoken could be achieved. The basis of Weizmann's great chemical discoveries had lain in the translation of solar energy, through the organic processes of plant life, to human use. Applying this thinking to the positive physical qualities of Palestine could be a fascinating exercise. The country might be tiny and arid, but it had the River Jordan and the sun. All that was needed was a way to harness both. Seen in this light, the argument for increased Jewish immigration was not so much a Jewish imperative as a means of providing the labour and energy with which to tame the environment in order to create wealth and a higher standard of living for both the races that lived in Palestine.

Having made these points, Weizmann sat back and smiled. He had made his case for the Jews' being allowed to continue to live in Palestine, and he had reminded his guest that the Jews were the ones with the ability to develop the land for the benefit of all: more malarial swampland could be cleared and drained, to be replaced by fertile farmland; land that had lain derelict for generations had already been transformed into green settlements. As the country became more prosperous and both sides benefited from the prosperity, hostile feelings would vanish. In the seven relatively peaceful years of immigration between 1922 and 1929, the painful transition from backward to progressive economy had already started.

Major mistakes, however, made by both sides, had undermined this process. Each side had underestimated the power of the religious and cultural divide. Time and again attempts had been made to create joint institutions, from schools to trade unions, but it never seemed possible to bridge the gap. When attempts were made to link the unions, for example, they were defeated by Jewish refusal to accept a wage policy which would reduce their standard of living to that of the Arabs; and in the years of unemployment, Jews insisted on their quota of jobs in public works.

Nevertheless, as he continued his conversation with the Commissioner, Weizmann enlarged on his theme of the future of Palestine. In his view, he repeated for emphasis, the core of success lay in a large Jewish immigrant labour force uniting with the Arab farmers to exploit the potential of the land.

The Commissioner sat back and watched the sun finally sink below the distant horizon. He had had a long and tiring journey, and although he was still impressed by Weizmann's arguments, doubts had begun to creep into his mind. Weizmann's ideas were all very well in theory, but the obstacles that had to be faced before they could be put into practice were legion, and whether Arab–Jewish collaboration could ever be brought to the point Weizmann described seemed very questionable indeed. As was the idea of a vast army of Jewish immigrants heading for the rural areas to farm and develop them. Most of the latest immigrants were city-dwellers and wanted to remain so, making for Tel Aviv with quite different ambitions. They wanted to open businesses in the rapidly expanding town.

On 25 November, Weizmann presented his argument to the Peel Commission. He made such a good case for Jewish immigration, and in such stirring terms, that for a moment the Arab Higher Commission had second thoughts about their decision to boycott. After a stormy session, they decided to maintain their non-co-operative stance, though they also arranged to send the former mayor of Jerusalem, Ragheb Bey Al-Nashashibi, to Amman, which was to be the Peel Commission's next port of call.

As their visit to Jerusalem approached its end, most of the Commissioners expressed disappointment that they had not had enough time to listen fully to all the various groups who wished to register their opinions. In fact the year ended on a somewhat sour note when the Russian-born Jewish representative Dov Hos was interviewed by the Commission. Years earlier, he had been sentenced to death by the Turks for defending Jewish settlements against Arab attack. He'd escaped, and later joined the British Army. The Commission asked him general questions about the foundation of a variety of new institutions in Palestine, and in reply he described how the Jews had helped save money for the British government by themselves funding the establishment of a number of schools and hospitals.

For some reason this gave offence to Sir Horace Rumbold, the former Ambassador to Berlin, who, his face red with anger, leant across his desk and bellowed, "Now let me tell you this! Lord Cromer was in Egypt for twenty-five years. When he arrived, the country was in a very bad way indeed; but by the end of his term he had restored it to prosperity!"

Rumbold went on to explain how he felt that the task in Palestine would present even greater problems than those in Egypt had presented to Cromer. Palestine had been in an even worse state than Egypt was when the British took over: "Not only was this country completely derelict . . . but the Mandatory Power has had to develop [it] having regard to a unique experiment, the injection of an alien race into the body politic of this native race."

The Jews were furious. How dare anyone refer to them as an "alien race"? "The Jews have brought to this country possibilities that have never existed before," declared Dov Hos.

It was sad not to end the year on a more positive note, but most of those attending the New Year's Eve dance at the King David Hotel felt that little had been achieved. There remained one rather surreal incident. As the Commission's Secretary, John Martin, wrote in a private letter home, Sir Horace Rumbold was in for "a rude reminder" of his discourtesy. Sir Horace was in a deep sleep in his room when a young woman burst in and blew a small trumpet loudly in his ear. He awoke with a start to find her yelling at him that he was "the ugliest member of the Commission". She continued to blow the trumpet and to express her opinion of the Commission and everyone connected with it; and she left little doubt of how she felt about the cowering figure of Sir Horace, who had retreated beneath the bedclothes.

Early in the New Year, however, the Arabs decided to end their boycott of the Commission after all and sent Haj Amin el Husseini, the Mufti of Jerusalem, as their first representative. Haj Amin was hardly likely to take a liberal view. It was he who had established the Arab Higher Committee at the start of the Intifada, and he who controlled and encouraged strikes among the Arab workforce.

During his interview, he explained how the Balfour Declaration had favoured the Jewish settlers. Since the time it was signed, the Jews had acquired large tracts of Arab land, and those in the most fertile parts of the country, he alleged. He appealed for the Balfour Declaration to be annulled and for Palestine to be created a sovereign Arab state. When asked what he felt should happen to the 400,000 Jews already living in the country, he replied without hesitation that Palestine was in no position to "assimilate and digest" them. When he was further asked if he would have preferred Turkey as Mandatory Power, rather than Britain, he answered that the Arabs of Palestine would prefer above all "complete independence". The Commissioners listened to him carefully, but his arguments did not sway them. It was clear to them that this powerful representative of his people was responsible for most of the problems which had called the Commission into existence in the first place. They reminded him that they believed that he and the Arab Higher Committee had been "responsible for extending and protracting the strikes", and for refusing to condemn "the acts of sabotage and terrorism which became more frequent as the strikes continued".

As the Commissioners prepared to leave the country, uppermost in their minds was one fact: the days of the Balfour Declaration were over. Jews and Arabs were living in a different world. The twenty years since the Declaration had seen dramatic changes in Palestine. Then, it had been an underpopulated backwater; now, it was a crowded territory seething with energy and discontent, and the current racial and political situation was not helped by daily broadcasts in Arabic of anti-Semitic propaganda from Mussolini's Italy.

The Jews had developed the country and wanted to go on doing so. But the Arabs had historic rights of residency, too, and their Muslim neighbours had oil – a commodity the West could not afford to ignore. Anxious to remain on good terms with the neighbouring Arab states for fear of losing potential suppliers, and sharpened by the threat of Hitler, the British took a consistently conciliatory line with them. Oil gave its owners the trump card.

In July 1937, the Peel Commission published its findings. What was needed was a new mandate. Arab and Jewish interests could not be reconciled, and therefore the only answer was the partition of the country.

David Ben-Gurion, though not without misgivings, agreed with the Commission. At least this solution would pave the way more quickly for a formal Jewish state, and there was no reason why Arab and Jew should not live side by side in peace, even if they could not do so together. The Peel Commission recommended that the Jews should be given the

2,000 square miles that covered the coastal plain, the Jezreel Valley and Galilee, while the Arabs would get the remainder of Palestine, with the exception of Jerusalem which, with its religious significance for Christian, Jew and Muslim alike, would continue to be an internationally recognised city, free for all to come and worship as they wished.

The Jews were not happy. The area allotted to them was small, hardly large enough for the future immigration that they'd hoped for; but they shared Ben-Gurion's view that any state which was clearly theirs was better than none. At least the plan would give them the freedom to control the flow of immigration; and the news from Germany was ever darker. So, the Zionist Congress gave the plan its qualified acceptance.

The Arabs, however, rejected it out of hand. They viewed it as a compromise, and the Arab Higher Committee, led by Haj Amin el Husseini, stepped up its terror campaign in order to force the British to accede to the idea of making Palestine an Arab state, *tout court*.

In the first weeks of March 1938, a number of Jews were murdered in Galilee; then three more were killed in an Arab bomb attack. This time the Jews struck back. Within hours, the Irgun hit two Arab cafés in Jerusalem with bombs, killing one man and injuring twenty more. This action was immediately condemned by the Jewish Agency, which appealed to all Jews to have nothing to do with reprisals. The British, in no doubt about the identity of the main agitator, decided to arrest the Mufti and remove him from the scene of his activities. But Haj Amin was forewarned of their intention and took sanctuary on the sacred Haram esh Sharif in Jerusalem. Not wishing to offend worldwide Muslim sensibilities by breaking the sanctuary, the British withdrew, but cordoned the area off, giving police orders to take Amin prisoner the moment he left the holy ground.

The violence continued. In September, the British District Commissioner in Galilee was murdered. The Mandatory Authority immediately stripped the Mufti of his positions as President of the Supreme Muslim Council and Chairman of the General Wakf Committee, which was responsible for all Muslim religious property. The following day, Arab youths forced all Muslim shopkeepers in Jerusalem to close their doors in protest. Meanwhile, the British waited at the gates of Haram esh Sharif for Haj Amin to come out. One night in October 1938, he slipped past the police, disguised as a woman. He remained in hiding for some time, finally making his way to Beirut. During the Second World War he lived in Germany, meeting Hitler, Ribbentrop and other Nazi leaders on various occasions and attempting to co-ordinate Arab and Nazi policies in the Middle East. This softly spoken, courteous man, the most implacable fighter for the Arab cause, never set foot in Palestine again.

Although the Mufti had gone, the killings continued. Nine days after Amin had vanished, the son of an eminent Jerusalem Jew, David Yellin, was shot dead as he left his office. Outraged members of the Irgun threatened to take vengeance, despite further calls from the Jewish Agency for restraint. In the second week of November, the killing of five more Jews working in a quarry at Kiryat Anavim angered the Irgun to the point where they could contain themselves no longer. Seven Arabs were murdered in retaliation.

Few Jews supported Irgun reprisals. The majority still felt that violent reaction was not the answer. The Jewish Agency called a meeting on the day the Irgun killings took place to condemn terrorism and to express their disapproval of the action. However there was one dissenting voice: the Romanian-born Judah Leib Fishman declared that every Jew had the right to bear arms "in his own defence".

The British Government consigned the Peel Commission's report to a bottom drawer. And in Palestine, once again rioters invaded the streets.

Chapter Twelve: The Gathering Storm

On 19 September 1938, the British and the French governments, acting well beyond their remits, effectively obliged the Czechoslovak regime to hand over to Hitler all of its territory in which more than half the citizens were Sudeten Germans. The cession of the Sudetenland to Hitler was a disastrous tactical error and an impardonable interference in Czechoslovakia's internal affairs, but Prime Ministers Neville Chamberlain and Edouard Daladier were desperate to avoid an all-out war, and for Chamberlain especially no price was too high. When Britain could have nipped Hitler's ambitions in the bud, Chamberlain allowed them to flourish.

The British clung to the belief that Hitler was a reasonable man who would abide by international law and could be contained if his local territorial demands were humoured. This belief affected their foreign policy in treating with the Jews and Arabs of Palestine. Convinced that they could still persuade the two sides to live in peace, they convened a Peace Conference at St James's Palace in London early in 1939. The Jewish delegation included Ben-Gurion, Chaim Weizmann, Berl Katznelson and Yitzhak Ben-Zvi.

Assembled in a glittering hall, hung with magnificent chandeliers and portraits of the great and the good of British history, the meeting got off to a bad start. The Arabs refused to sit down with the Jews at all, so there had to be two separate addresses of welcome. As if that were not ominous enough, the Colonial Secretary, Malcolm MacDonald, then delivered a statement, the sense of which would later be translated into the White Paper of 1939 to which I have already referred. It will be remembered that this limited Jewish immigration to a maximum of 15,000 per year for 1939 and the following five years, after which all immigration would cease unless the Arabs agreed to an extension. In addition, the rights of Jews to buy land were drastically curtailed.

The White Paper quickly became known to the Palestine Jews as the Black Paper. It could not have been more obvious that the British were heavily biased towards Arab interests, hoping thereby both to safeguard their stake elsewhere in the Middle East and to control or at least influence where the Arab oil went. The Jews naturally rejected the White Paper. In its response, the Jewish Agency recorded that "It is in the darkest hour of Jewish history that the British Government proposes to deprive the Jews of their last hope and to close the road back to their Homeland. It is a cruel blow, doubly cruel because it comes from the government of a great nation which has extended a helping hand to the Jews, and whose position must rest on foundations of moral authority and international good faith."

The Arabs also rejected the Paper. For them, it did not go far enough. They wanted Palestine to be declared an Arab state at once, an immediate cessation of Jewish immigration and a review of the status of every single Jewish immigrant since 1918. Had the British agreed to that, a bloodbath would have been inevitable; but since most Arab states sided with the Germans at the time, MacDonald's statement was all the more surprising to the Jews at the Conference. After the Colonial Secretary had read the statement, Ben-Gurion rose and addressed him in a firm voice, clearly only just managing to keep his anger under control: "Permit me to say that the restriction of Jewish immigration will prove impossible without the aid of British bayonets . . . It will likewise be impossible to convert Palestine into an Arab state against Jewish opposition without the continuous support of British bayonets."

Naturally such a comment did nothing to divert Britain

from its stated course of action, though the White Paper
was immediately condemned by Winston Churchill as "a ˄
plain breach of a solemn obligation". Ben-Gurion flew back
to Jerusalem and there, at a general meeting of the Zionist
Council, he roared, "We go forth to smite the policy of the
White Paper, and let us not be found wanting!" The Jews of
Palestine rallied to his cry.

Jona Rosenfeld found the news devastating. She was dedicated
to her new home and had by now joined the Haganah. When the
contents of the White Paper were made public, she wasted no
time in going out into the streets to protest:

> We shouted and paraded. I participated as one of the crowd. I couldn't
> help thinking how different our marches were from the Brownshirt
> *Fackelzug* that I had seen back in Germany. Here, we were protesting
> legally against a legal authority, and, unlike the SA, we were doing it
> without songs or blazing torches. Yet we had a feeling of unity, of
> belonging together.
>
> I had nothing against the British personally. In fact, I had got to
> know many of them quite well. Behind our house there was a large
> polo ground where the British soldiers played. I befriended many
> of them. Not far away was a cemetery for Indian soldiers. That
> was where the British tommies took prostitutes, and sometimes we
> sneaked a look at what went on there. So I had some contact with
> the British. But when it came to a protest like this I still went along
> with the crowd.

One initially peaceful demonstration degenerated into a riot
when several hundred Jewish youths descended on Zion Square
and ran amok, breaking shop windows, tearing down lamp-posts
and smashing telephone kiosks. Some of the crowd made their
way to the immigration and citizenship offices and, in a bid to
destroy the records contained there, set part of the building on
fire. The British police responded with baton charges in which
over 100 Jews were injured. Then shots were fired from the
Jewish side which mortally wounded one constable, Harold
Lawrence.

Furious at the death of the British policeman, the GOC British
Forces summoned the Jewish leadership to his office and warned

them that "There will be no more rioting in Jerusalem; but if blood is shed, that blood will be on the heads of the Jews." The Jewish leaders took note. The following night, Ben-Zvi, facing a crowd of 1,000 angry young people in Zion Square as Chairman of the General Council of Palestine Jews, was able to persuade them to disperse peacefully. Two more days of marches and demonstrations, however, resulted in a second warning that any breaches of the peace would be met with force. Following that statement, uniformed Jewish special constables appeared on the streets, wearing brown berets and khaki uniforms, ready to keep order.

Time was running out for the Jews of Europe, although there were many who found it hard to face the fact. Sam Bresler, from Radom near Warsaw, was well aware of the hatred the Poles had for the Jews:

> There were 80,000 people living in the city and 34,000 of them were Jews. The Jews had been hated in Poland for centuries, but my family, which was well off, lived in a Jewish quarter, so we were sheltered from the worst of it. Then suddenly we began to hear the name Hitler, and refugees started to come into Poland from Germany. Things went from bad to worse after that. In 1938, my aunt came over on a visit from Canada. We were all sitting round the dining-room table one day when my mother said, "Maybe it's time for us to move to Canada." My aunt was surprised. "What for, Sara?" she asked. "Here, you have three maids. In Calgary, *I'm* a maid!"

Even as a child, growing up in Berlin, Miriam Spielman had talked about Israel. She always knew that someday she would live there. Then, early in November 1938, came *Kristallnacht*, the "Night of Broken Glass". In a so-called "spontaneous" reaction to the assassination of a minor German diplomat in Paris by a young Jew protesting at the treatment of his people by the Polish and German governments, Jewish shops and businesses throughout Germany were attacked. If the message hadn't been clear to the Jews of Germany before, *Kristallnacht* made it so. Miriam Spielman remembers . . .

... the terrible attacks that were being made on Jewish property, and the breaking of the shop windows ... I left Germany soon afterwards on what was called a children's transport. Only children were allowed to leave Germany at that time, without their parents; and then only children who had Polish citizenship, which luckily for me I had. My grandfather was a Pole, and as soon as he saw what was going on in Berlin he went and got me a Polish passport – this was just weeks before everything exploded in *Kristallnacht.*

I had an older sister who had left much earlier for Israel on a certificate. I was too young at the time to go with her. When the time came for me to leave, everything happened very fast indeed. I didn't even have time to say goodbye to my parents. I was just told that it was time to go, and that was it. We were put on a train to Holland and sailed from the Hook to Harwich in England. Once we'd arrived there, we were put up in a big tent at Dovercourt nearby. There, we were lined up, and various Englishwomen arrived and chose which children they would look after. A group of us was taken to London, where a hostel had been started for us. I was fifteen by then, and I decided to take a correspondence course in Hebrew. There was a Jewish college which sent out the tests: you answered a series of questions and they sent you more tests. And that's how I learnt Hebrew.

One day they wrote a letter to say that they were having a competition. There was to be a writing contest and the thirty best essays would win the prize of going to Palestine for a visit. So I went in for it and wrote a composition on "Why I want to go to a kibbutz".

I won. Once in Palestine, I had no intention of coming back. I had an uncle in England and I told him all about my plans. He was delighted for me and gave me money for the trip.

The mother of Dr Elihy Hoffman got her family out of Germany. Young Elihy was keen to go:

Being a Zionist, sure, I wanted to go. I was only fifteen years old, but I was pretty advanced politically. I wanted to escape, even though this was still before 1938, and things in Germany were still fairly normal for the Jews. I took a crash course in Hebrew in order to prepare myself, and I took to the language well. When the time came to leave – in July 1939 – I was ready.

I was attached to a youth group which had arranged the date of departure and bought the tickets and so on. On 10 July we left for Berlin by train. It may sound strange, but the few belongings, like books and so forth, that I sent on ahead, all arrived safely.

The train journey, which took five hours, was unlike the one I'd taken to Berlin once before with my mother. On that occasion we'd been joined in our compartment by two SS men. I'd looked at them with such hatred that my mother poked me in the ribs and whispered, "You look out of the window."

Our group made its way to Trieste, and there we boarded a ship. As it was still peacetime, the voyage was uneventful and we had fun, singing and dancing. Once we'd arrived in Palestine and I'd got settled, I liked what I found. Tel Aviv in those days was simple and uncomplicated. The people were pretty open and there was no formality about them. I especially enjoyed the openness and the facilities of the school I went to. The staff were excellent. There was a library which was second to none. In the afternoons, you could sit and read in almost any language you chose. Once a year there was an opera, performed by the school orchestra and the children of the school.

It really was a fantastic school. The children were from the cream of society, yet there was no class distinction at all. I arrived as a poor German Jew, but I had no problem with being accepted. Ben-Gurion's daughter was in my class, yet no distinction was made between her and me. The only difference was that I had yet to speak Hebrew really fluently; but they knew this and accepted it.

The biggest difference, compared with Europe, was that the pressures we'd had from outside dangers no longer existed. I was lucky enough to be able to write to my mother via a friend in Switzerland, and eventually I found out that she, too, was on her way. Meanwhile the relatives with whom I was staying arranged for me to complete my education with two years' practical training in building.

Gradually and reluctantly, the Jews of Europe began to leave the countries their people had lived in for up to 1,000 years. Those who left first lived in the countries first occupied by the Nazis – Austria and the Sudetenland. Soon, rotting and verminous ships from the Danube, laden with Jews, began to leave various seaports.

The Jews aboard had parted with princely sums to the Nazis and the ships' owners in exchange for this means of escape. Crushed together, the refugees struggled to survive the nightmarish journey to their homeland, most limping ashore near Haifa under cover of night to avoid being turned back by the Mandatory Authority, whose immigration laws forbade them entry.

Liesl Katz was born in Austria, where she spent her youth. Aware of her Jewish heritage, she was nevertheless proud to be an Austrian:

My father was a very well-known journalist in Vienna, and when Hitler took over Austria in 1938 my father was among the prominent people of the Jewish faith who were taken into custody – this was so-called "protective custody" – they were not sent to a camp. He was released on 9 June, and three months later he signed an undertaking that he and his family would leave Austria. We were very fortunate because as my father had always had a connection with Jewish sporting organisations he was able to get a visa to go to Palestine legally.

Soon afterwards, my mother, my father and I (I was fourteen at the time) packed our bags and left. I was an only child, and I was very excited about going to Palestine. We took a train to Trieste, where we spent the night in a dormitory in a hostel. Two ships left for Palestine each week. When we were there, one was called the *Palestine* and the other the *Galilee*.

We had not been permitted to take any money out of Austria except for the equivalent of £5 per person; but we were allowed to take a containerload of furniture and personal belongings. My father's brother and his family – his wife and two children – had left Austria two or three weeks earlier, and they had already rented a four-room flat in Tel Aviv by the time we arrived, so we had somewhere to live. We travelled with our container so we were able to furnish our rooms in the flat immediately; but since the container cost £15 to clear customs, getting our belongings cleaned us out of our money completely.

My father, who spoke French and English as well as German, found it difficult to learn another language, and so could not work as a journalist any more. My mother, who was then not quite thirty-four years old, had never worked before, but she and her sister-in-law started a small restaurant in the flat, preparing lunches. Most of our customers were new immigrants, and I remember that at that time most of them worked as pickers in the orange groves. They got a three-course lunch, with camel meat, which tasted fine.

As it became increasingly apparent that British sympathy lay with the Arabs, so the Jewish leadership agreed that their people must be in a position to defend themselves firmly both at the negotiating table and in the field. The Haganah grew in strength. Nevertheless, it seemed to most Jews that Chamberlain made a habit of appeasing those who posed the greatest threat. In May 1939, through the White Paper, the Chamberlain Government had given in to the Arabs (as the Jews saw it) in the same way that it had given in to Hitler: when Chamberlain had shaken hands with Hitler in Munich at the end of September 1938 and by so doing sealed Czechoslovakia's fate (and, had he but known it, that of the rest of the world), his action had signalled to the Palestine Jews that they could have little hope of support from such a man.

The Irgun was attracting attention overseas with its policy of reprisal. It hit the headlines in 1938 when a young member of the force, Shlomo Ben-Yosef, was sentenced to death by the British for his part in an attack on a bus. The strike was made in retaliation against an Arab attack on a car which had left two women and a child dead. Although there were no casualties on the bus, the British were determined to make an example of the Irgun members involved.

The three youths who were arrested were accused of the illegal possession of arms. Two were sentenced to death, but only Ben-Yosef was hanged, even though appeals for clemency came in from all around the world. He was the first Jew to be hanged in Palestine. Four years later, in 1942, three British policemen rushed to the site of an explosion at a Tel Aviv flat. As they broke down the door, a second bomb exploded, killing all three: it had been a trap. One of the officers was the man who had hanged Ben-Yosef.

Despite all the setbacks, more and more Jews were getting into the Promised Land, and the Jewish population climbed to 440,000. The White Paper restrictions reinforced Jewish

determination to stay and to defend their right to stay; and
those who were already there did everything they could to help
newcomers bypass the immigration quotas. Although 1939 was
a year of anxiety, it continued to see new arrivals. The newly
wed Bianca Romano-Segre and her husband were set to begin
a new life in Tel Aviv:

> We were taken first to a big hut. In the middle of it were donkeys and
> camels and birds. It was a very strange place, and we began to think
> that coming here had been a terrible mistake. We took a carriage
> from there to what they called a hotel. It was dreadful! Worst of all
> was the fact that there were very few Italians in Palestine at that time;
> and added to that was the problem of how to earn a living. I had
> my school diploma, and my husband was a lawyer – but that wasn't
> much good to him here, and he was reluctant to learn Hebrew.

They were luckier than most. The White Paper of 1939
effectively ended the British Mandate's authority in the eyes
of the Jews; and its severe quota restriction ended the hopes
of millions of fellow Jews trapped in a Europe over which the
shadow of National Socialism was falling rapidly. Furthermore,
the land-purchase restriction made it increasingly difficult to
accommodate those Jews who could get into Palestine; and
land-purchase laws were harder to circumvent than immigration
controls.

What was to be done? Events in Europe occupied the world's
attention, and the small strip of land at the eastern end of the
Mediterranean was of little importance to anyone except those
who inhabited it. The British were aware that the Jews would not
take the conditions of the White Paper lying down; but although
they realised the potential danger inherent in this, they were no
longer interested in actively supporting the Jewish cause; thus
it was clear to the Palestine Jews that they would have to fight
their own corner for themselves and by themselves.

They did what they could, but without greater official
status or political clout than they had, it was impossible
to convince Britain that Palestine was the only country to
provide a refuge for the persecuted Jews of Europe. It will be
remembered that virtually no other state offered unconditional

Immigrants at
Jaffa port,
November 1933.

One of the first groups of Aliyah children arriving in Haifa, February 1934.

Beit Lid immigrant camp (*ma'abara*), January 1950.

or unlimited sanctuary to the Jews, and in the course of time only Denmark among the occupied countries comported itself with any honour in respect of its Jewish citizens. There, when the Nazi edict came for all Jews to wear the yellow Star of David, the entire population did so, including King Christian X, making it impossible for the Germans to distinguish between Gentile and Jew. Denmark later managed to ferry all its Jews to safety in Sweden. Australia, Canada and the USA accepted some immigrants, but by no means enough, or quickly enough, to avert the slaughter that was to come. Closer to home, the excuse that there were insufficient ships to transport the Jews out of Europe hardly stood up at a time when the shipbuilding industry had never been so active.

In the exodus that preceded the Holocaust, many strange stories of coincidence and miraculous deliverance abound. The parents of one unnamed Polish teenager encouraged her to leave and make her way to Palestine while there was still time. Leaving her loved ones was a painful experience, but without her father's parting gift her escape would not have succeeded:

As we stood in the centre of our village street, I hugged my crying mother and then turned to my father, who held out a small gift: it was a cheap, bright red cover for my passport.

After a few hours of walking, I arrived at the border control post. Although the war had yet to start, the guards were already sympathetic to the Nazi cause. I handed one of them my passport. He laughed and threw it into a room behind him, telling me to return some hours later, which I did. Once again I faced the same guard and asked for my passport back. He jerked his thumb in the direction of the room behind him. It was piled high with passports – all of them belonging to people who were, like me, trying to get out. "If you can find your passport in half an hour, you can leave," he sneered.

I was horrified; but I went into the room and there, sticking out among all the hundreds of other passports, was one with a bright red cover. I snatched it from the pile and handed it to the guard, who at least was as good as his word and allowed me to go. I wish my mother and father could have seen that, without their little parting gift, I would never have made it to

Israel. But they never knew, and they never will. They died in a concentration camp.

Elihy Hoffman's father never considered leaving Germany; but after his death in 1935, his widow had other ideas. Elihy remembers:

> We knew about Palestine because we had relatives living there. The main idea at the time was to get me a student certificate which would allow me to go to school in Tel Aviv. It took my mother three years, from 1936 until 1939, to get that certificate for me. I went to Palestine in 1939, as I've told you, and in the same year my eight-year-old sister went on a *Kindertransport* to England. My mother wasn't able to get away until 1941, but then she managed to reach Haifa by the Black Sea route.

Despite all his efforts, Chamberlain was unable to avoid conflict, and when Hitler at last invaded Poland – with whom Britain had signed a treaty – at the beginning of September 1939, he declared war on Germany. But the German invasion of Poland left millions of Jews trapped. Those living in west Poland made a frantic effort to escape, but they soon found their last remaining route to freedom cut off as the German armies advanced across Belgium, the Netherlands and France. Soon, Britain was standing alone against the most brutal dictator the world had ever seen. Men and women rushed forward to join the armed services. Amongst those who joined the British Army was London-born Lewis Harris. His wartime career would lead him to Palestine for the first time:

> I joined the British Army in 1939. I started as a private and finished as a major. I was in Palestine three times during the war. It was like an oasis – a refuge from the conflict. On one of my journeys there, I met my wife-to-be, who was also in the Army, in the ATS. That was in 1943, and I had just crossed the desert from Baghdad, along the pipeline. I had come from some of the most godforsaken places in the war, and arriving here was wonderful. The girls were beautiful, they wore very little and the sun shone. How could I fail to be impressed with Palestine? The whole experience of it made me a Zionist.

Britain's refusal to help the Jews of Europe by lifting immigration restrictions placed many of the Jews living in the homeland in a cleft stick. Torn between anger over the White Paper and wanting to help Britain in its fight against Nazi Germany, many young Palestine Jews put aside their differences and volunteered for the British forces. Soon 19,000 of them, of whom 10 per cent were women, were in British uniform.

It hadn't been easy for them to swallow their disagreement with the British and fight side by side against a common enemy, but most believed that, faced with the evil that was enveloping Europe, the fight on the home front could wait. And had not Hitler specifically declared war on the Jews? Tensions, however, between the British and the Palestine Jews remained, and were heightened by such tragic events as the sinking of the *Patria* in November 1940. The *Patria* was a refugee ship which the British were in the process of sending from the port of Haifa to Mauritius. Members of the Irgun had smuggled themselves aboard and were trying to disable the ship's engines in order to oblige the authorities to allow the refugees to land. In the attempt, however, they accidentally blew a hole in the hull, and the *Patria* went down just offshore. Among the survivors was Temima Hillel:

In September 1940, four ships finally sailed up the Danube to take us to Palestine. They were crowded with Jewish refugees from Czechoslovakia, Germany and Austria. We boarded the *Uranus*, a vessel with room for perhaps 300 people. There were over 1,000 of us on board.

The journey down the Danube into Romania was calm, but even so my sister was terribly seasick. We took about a week to reach the sea. We sailed on to Tulcea and then transferred to two ocean-going ships, the *Pacific*, which we boarded, and the *Milus*. Again, we were desperately overcrowded and we spent three weeks moored off Tulcea. No one seemed to know why, although rumours flew around the ship. My family had a tiny cabin next door to the lavatories. The smell was terrible, and it was months before I got it out of my nostrils.

We had relatives in Romania, and they brought us boxes of food during those three weeks. I remember eating soup and sardines. Those same relatives were later sent to the death camps.

Finally, we set sail. We were very afraid. It was wartime by then, and we were in fear of attack by submarines. The journey took a week or ten days. We ran out of fuel on the high seas and the ship was stripped of all its wood – the bunks, the railings, whatever we could find to burn, to power the engines.

At last we approached Palestine. We were told we'd have to land secretly at night to evade the British. I was really scared at that, and when the British stopped us at sea I remember being glad, because that meant that we wouldn't have to make a secret night landing on a beach. The British gave us oranges and towed us into the port of Haifa – once again we had run out of fuel.

We stayed on board at Haifa for several days, and once again rumours began to fly. Then we learnt that the British planned to deport us to Mauritius. This was very hard to bear. It had taken us so long to reach Eretz Israël. We could see the lights of Haifa. Still they wouldn't let us land.

We were transferred to another ship for the journey to Mauritius. This was the *Patria*. She was a beautiful passenger liner, but once again we were desperately overcrowded on board. There were the 1,500 or so people from the *Pacific*, and to them they added all the people from the *Milus*, which had been stopped too. In the end there were about 3,600 of us – a massive number for a ship of that size. And then once again we sat in port and waited.

On the day of the explosion I awoke feeling unwell. I remember that I was wearing a beautiful pink nightie with flowers on it. It was still early in the morning when we heard and felt the explosion. I was still in bed. From my porthole I could see people, mostly young people, jumping into the water. The ship had already begun to list badly, and within fifteen minutes one side – our side – was completely under water. We were fighting our way up the sloping gangway by then. My father lost his grip and slid back into the water, up to his neck. He called out to my mother, my sister and me to save ourselves. There was nothing we could do to help him. As we moved on, we heard him saying the *Sheme Yisroël*.

Somehow we managed to scramble up on deck. It was full of British soldiers. No one seemed to know what had happened to the ship, but they did all they could to help us. My mother even got one of them to take a rope and go back with her to try to help my father, and together they saved him. Meanwhile, I was holding on to a rail to stop myself from sliding across the deck into the water. A British soldier managed to make his way to me and held me safe. All I could think about was my father. I thought he had drowned. Then we were lowered into a lifeboat, but as I got in a nail that was sticking out ripped my beautiful nightie, and through it my buttock and my thigh. My sister was screaming and I can remember telling her to stop. "Screaming won't help," I said.

When we got to shore they put us in a huge barn of a place, along with the other survivors, and brought us clothes. I chose a pair of Bermuda shorts and a blouse. We started searching for our parents, but it was several hours before we found them safe, as well as two aunts who'd been on board with us. All six of us had survived.

Some 260 people drowned on the *Patria* that day. Among them was the woman I'd studied Hebrew with in Bratislava.

Faced with the decision to help the British fight the Nazis despite the White Paper, David Ben-Gurion responded with his usual pragmatism: "We shall fight the war as if there were no White Paper," he declared, "but we shall fight the White Paper as if there were no war."

He lost no opportunity of publicising the role now being played by thousands of Jews in the British armed forces. They were fighting gallantly alongside their Allied comrades; crack Jewish paratroopers were dropping behind enemy lines; and Jewish soldiers risked far more than their Gentile brothers-in-arms: as Jews, they could face the concentration camps if captured. To spare British resources in Palestine which were badly needed elsewhere, the Haganah volunteered to deal with the riots stirred up by the pro-Nazi regimes of Iraq and Syria.

In 1940 Ben-Gurion returned to London once more and took a room within walking distance of his small office in the Jewish Agency building close to Regent's Park. It was the time when the Blitzkrieg had started in deadly earnest, so he was able to experience at first hand some of the brutality of the Nazis.

Although the bombing of London was uppermost in the minds of everyone in the city, Ben-Gurion's mission was to try to persuade the British to allow the Jews of Palestine to fight back against Arab aggression. His plea for the foundation of a Jewish Legion was turned down. Undaunted, he flew to

America. The USA had yet to enter the war, but Ben-Gurion was convinced that they would be just as opposed to the White Paper as he was, once the contents were known. Leading political figures there listened to him sympathetically, but that was not enough for Ben-Gurion. At a mass rally in Carnegie Hall in New York, he denounced the White Paper roundly in the course of a passionate speech soliciting support for the Jewish homeland. He described the boat-loads of would-be immigrants frustrated in their attempts to reach Palestine, the sinking of the *Patria* and the fate of the Jews left at the mercy of the Nazis.

Unfortunately, the world had suddenly turned away from the Jewish plight. Most people felt that they had enough problems of their own. They believed, too, that the reports coming out of Europe were exaggerated.

Meanwhile, the Jews of Palestine had to face the continuing threat of Arab aggression. They were still greatly outnumbered, yet every day saw the arrival of more immigrants, and most of them were young. Some as young as thirteen were becoming members of youth groups which combined military training with daily lessons. For several hours a day, Haganah training sessions included the use of a pistol and how to carry out guard duties – skills which would prove invaluable to the many settlements in isolated areas. The schools themselves were vulnerable to attack, and many took on the appearance of fortresses, rather than places of learning. At the same time, children who had just arrived had to face all the problems of settling in, making new friends and learning Hebrew.

The fact that Liesl Katz now lived away from her beloved Vienna made her a very unhappy schoolgirl. Like others who had immigrated, she remained homesick despite the dreadful stories which were filtering out of Europe:

> I had always been good at school, but I was under a cloud when I started again in Tel Aviv. My parents couldn't afford private Hebrew lessons for me, and that made me very sad.
>
> One day I had an especially unhappy experience. Every Friday, some of the children would go round with collection boxes. A certain teacher used to send me round with them, until one Friday when I told him, "I'm sorry, I can't do it today because some friends are

arriving from Europe and they're coming to our house." In front of the whole class he shouted back, "What do you mean, you can't? Don't you know that you're only here in the first place because we have helped to shelter you?" I turned pale and I was very frightened by what he'd said. I went and sat down.

Later, when I got home, I told my mother what had happened. My father was furious and complained to the headmaster. The teacher was made to apologise to me, but I couldn't stand the place any more and so I left that school.

I remained very unhappy. My parents had no time left over for me, and the only outlet I had was with a youth group in a club where there were other German-speaking children. We used to go swimming – things like that. But my main problem was lack of contact with other children at school. Children can be very cruel and selfish, and they mocked me because I couldn't speak Hebrew.

I was very good at maths and physics, but the rest of my schooling was a disaster. I was so miserable and unhappy. I cried so much and I longed for Vienna. Hitler couldn't last forever, I thought; one day I'd be able to go back.

Far from her classroom, the Gestapo and the SS at work in Vienna were ensuring that the Jewish community of that city would be broken up in such a way that it would never recover from the blow they struck it then.

Chapter Thirteen: A Change of Heart

By spring 1941, the fortunes of war still continued to favour Hitler, and the members of the Haganah High Command were beginning to have serious doubts about the wisdom of allowing any more Palestine Jews to leave the country to serve in the British Army. Where would Palestine find those needed to defend the settlements from the Axis powers and the Arabs, if the Zionist leadership continued to allow their youth to disappear abroad?

The Haganah faced a more pressing problem as well. Although there was no question of the dedication of the young people who served in it, they still lacked the discipline and experience of a truly professional fighting force, since they had no proper training. Most of them performed only part-time duty in the Haganah, since they were also needed for work in the fields and the factories. To make matters worse, the Haganah was constantly criticised for failing to achieve its objectives; and this was compounded by the fact that an increasing number of people regarded them as draft-dodgers.

What was needed was an efficient, regular force which was well equipped, mobile and independent. Such a force would be answerable to the Haganah High Command and trained to carry out operations not only of a defensive nature. The Palmach – Hebrew for "shock brigades" – was developed in secret to meet these criteria. Led by the Russian Yitzhak Sadeh, it came into being at a time when the Jews of Palestine badly needed a morale boost.

Being accused of draft-dodging would not have bothered Hayim Hefer. He had joined the Haganah at the age of fourteen, and three years later went on to become a member of the new elite force:

> The whole Jewish population in the country at that time was under half a million, and we were surrounded by Arabs, so you had to watch your back wherever you went. I did combat training for about two years, spending half my time working on a kibbutz and the other half learning to use small arms, rifles and sten-guns.

Few knew it at the time, but the Jews were secretly beginning to chart the land they had moved into, and the cartographers and surveyors would soon be able to provide the Haganah with an invaluable new resource. Armed with detailed maps of the terrain in which they lived, they would be at a distinct advantage in any future battles. Hayim Hefer remembers:

> One chap in our group would often cheer us up when morale was low by saying that we weren't only being trained to find out where the enemy might be, but also the nature of the land in which he was.
>
> Most of the inhabitants of Galilee at the time were Arabs, and you had to be very sure before you went into an Arab village that the natives were friendly. And don't forget that they weren't our only enemies. As an underground organisation, we had to contend with the British police as well. So it was a little bit tricky. But I was a good scout. I remember walking back and forth across Galilee in four days, mapping the country all the time. I'd keep a lookout for paths and tracks and make sure I committed to memory exactly where they were, in case we ever needed to use them in the future. And my friends and I used the same techniques whenever we visited Arab villages, memorising and later noting down the best way in, the best way out, where the headman's house was, where the youth organisation HQ was – all the important things. We didn't have cameras then, so I learned how to draw. We had files on all the

villages, so that by the time the War of Independence broke out we had a good basis for our intelligence service.

I have an idea that the British knew what we were up to, but didn't think it that important – until we started blowing up their railway tracks and their police stations, that is.

Among the Jews of Palestine in the early 1940s morale was poor. Immigration had dropped back; at the same time there was widespread poverty, and unemployment was rising. It was certainly tough for Bianca Romano-Segre's husband. He'd been a lawyer in Italy, but as we've seen he had problems learning Hebrew and work in his field wasn't easy to find. In the end he decided to open an electrical supplies shop:

My husband sacrificed himself to that shop for twelve years. He hated it. Every minute of it. But while we ran the shop we also studied English – and in the end I took a degree. We also had some French, but not much.

I took on additional work painting pottery and lampshades for a big store in Tel Aviv; and we lived in a three-room flat. Our only problem was that we were a focus for all the Italians arriving at that time. So many came to eat and sleep at our little place that we could scarcely cope; but my husband was well known at home in Italy and there was no one else to take the newcomers in, so we did what we could. The result was that we played host to a succession of large families – up to five children, and they would stay for as long as a month sometimes. But the fact that our home became a kind of haven for so many people turned out to be very very useful later on when my husband switched careers and became a journalist.

Two or three months after Peter Gradenwitz arrived, the factory he'd found work in closed down because no one wanted to buy pianos. Luckily for him, the company kept their word and he was paid his full year's salary:

I found myself then travelling the country to various kibbutzim and giving lectures on music. I travelled by bus, but it was very dangerous because some of the roads were not safe; those that were safe were just as bumpy as the others, and I was constantly worried about my record collection, which I had to take everywhere with me and which was composed of 78s – very heavy and very breakable!

But it was an enjoyable way of meeting the people and seeing the country. I took to the younger people especially. I used to wonder why, what with the war in Europe and the threat that hung over us, they should take such an interest in my lectures; in the end I came to the conclusion that it was because they had so little to occupy their leisure time.

I remember one trip especially well. In the course of my talk at this particular kibbutz I told them about something that had happened during a performance of *Lohengrin* in Berlin. Lohengrin arrives on stage in a boat drawn by a swan, and sings an aria when he gets out which goes, "Thank you, my dear swan . . ." On that night the tenor suddenly disappeared – he'd fallen through an open trapdoor on the stage! When I reached this point a gentleman who'd been sitting in the front row turned very pale and left. After the lecture I tracked him down and asked him what had upset him. He told me that, on that night, he'd been the stage manager!

Meanwhile, as Hitler stepped up his war against the Jews, people still managed to find a way through the ever-closing net, and make the difficult journey to the haven of Palestine. Yaakov Edelstein was travelling with his parents from Poland on one of the most important days of his life:

I was about thirteen years old. We'd got on a train in Turkey which took us to Syria, and from there we went on to the Lebanon. One day we were forced to travel on *Shabat* – we had no choice. That Sabbath was also the day of my Bar-Mitzvah.

I had my *Drasha* [speech] all ready, because I thought we'd be staying in Lytta that day, not travelling at all. But on the train with us were several rabbis and *Yeshiva* students, so I stood up on a seat and gave my speech to them. It was about issues raised by the Talmud, and, according to tradition, the rabbis questioned me about my views on the passages from the Talmud I had chosen.

Many days later, we finally crossed the border into Palestine. We got down from the bus we were then travelling on, fell to the ground and kissed the soil of the homeland.

The homeland, however, was an uneasy place. Ben-Gurion's aim was to keep up pressure on the British to allow more immigrants in; but more importantly to see Hitler defeated before turning back to matters of domestic policy.

Far from everyone agreed with him. The underground army was unsure of its role. It had undertaken to control unrest in Palestine on behalf of the British, but any concessions it might have hoped for in return were not forthcoming. Should the Haganah therefore once more use force to put pressure on the British to relax the quotas? And if not, what should it do?

Officially barred from any form of retaliation against the British, the Zionist movement became a house divided against itself. The more Ben-Gurion urged restraint, the more radical elements of the Haganah turned away from him and towards underground organisations such as the Irgun and the even more extreme Stern Gang.

The pent-up frustrations of the past decade were about to explode.

Chapter Fourteen: Fortunes of War

The war was dragging into its third year, and the changes in Palestine were dramatic, as troops from around the world found themselves in a country which was new to most of them. For Bianca Romano-Segre, Tel Aviv in the early 1940s couldn't have been more different from the life she'd known in Milan:

To begin with, it was like a village; there were 60,000 people in all. And in the beginning, we liked the small flats, the small houses and indeed everything that was small. The Jewish population was very friendly and very warm.

The only unpleasant thing was to be unemployed; and it was hard not to be able to get more personal news from Europe than we did. At the outset, letters would still be coming in from all over – France, Germany, Spain . . . But then, after 1942, we only received letters via the Vatican and the Red Cross; and those letters were short – people were only permitted to send a ten-word greeting.

Unfortunately, I was unable to have children and that got me down a lot. But there was nothing to be done about it and, being free, I was able to do a lot of voluntary work – even for the British. Around that time they would ask Jewish women to invite English and Australian soldiers to tea. They came six at a time. They were always supposed to leave at 6 p.m., but often it was difficult for them to tear themselves away because it had been so long since they'd found themselves in domestic surroundings. Some of them had been fighting in the desert for two years, and they used to love to come round to chat with us. We took advantage of the occasion to make a bit of propaganda and tell them all about our plans for the future state of Israel; it was amazing how ignorant of us some of the soldiers were – not only the ones from India or South Africa, but even the British.

The influx of troops also meant increased employment opportunities. Liesl Katz's father managed to get a job at a British encampment:

And I found work as a dentist's assistant. My mother resuscitated her little restaurant, although most people didn't eat until about five o'clock because they all worked at the British camp, which was nearby. After a while, I got a job as a clerk in the NAAFI. I was very happy. I was seventeen and boyfriends were becoming a feature of my life! One of the nicest things was that we didn't have to speak Hebrew, which was still a bit of a strain: at work we spoke English, and most of my friends were German-speakers like me.

When Peter Gradenwitz realised that people could not go out to concerts because of the blackout restrictions, he decided to do something about it. His efforts were not without their attendant dangers, however:

I arranged gramophone record concerts from the roof of our apartment block. I remember that I'd received a set of rare recordings from the States, and I'd been to Jerusalem to present and play them on a radio programme. On the way back to Tel Aviv, we turned a corner in the road to find five Arabs standing there, pointing their rifles at us. My friend, who was driving, had a pistol in the car. He fired one shot at them and they ran away. All I could think of was how to protect my records. We holed up in a ditch for a while in case they decided to come back.

In May 1942, Ben-Gurion again flew to New York. His aim was unchanged: to make the case for a formal Jewish state to be established in Palestine.

The theatre of war had spread. Jews were fighting in each Allied army; but they had yet to have an army of their own in the field. For Ben-Gurion this was an added source of frustration. His people were suffering at the hands of the Germans, and they had a right to fight the enemy under their own flag. In an article addressed to the "free nations of the world", he held nothing back. "The Nazis deny us the right to live because we are Jews. Are the democracies to deny us the right to live and fight as Jews?" he wrote; and he was not alone in his belief. The head of the Political Department of the Zionist Executive in Jerusalem, Moshe Shertok (aka Sharett), and Chaim Weizmann joined their voices to Ben-Gurion's.

Together, they achieved their purpose. The Zionists were at last permitted to form a Jewish Brigade, which would serve as a unit of the British Army but wear their own insignia and fight under the blue and white flag of Israel. Within weeks of its formation, thousands of young Palestine Jews had stepped forward to join it. Its chief chaplain, the Englishman Rabbi Bernard Casperr, described its impact in his book, *With the Jewish Brigade*, published in 1947: big nations or empires might regard one brigade "as a small, almost insignificant affair. But to the Jewish people this formation . . . meant the fulfilment of our burning desire to stand up and fight back like a normal self-respecting people . . . There was not one among us who did not have the conviction that he was making history . . ."

The war in Europe continued, and gradually, after the USA had at last entered the arena and a few months later Germany had been defeated at Stalingrad, it became apparent that Hitler would lose. There was another general sigh of relief after D-Day, though not from the Jews, whose people continued to endure extreme torment. The Jews of Hungary were sent to Auschwitz in their hundreds of thousands *after* D-Day. The gas chambers of Auschwitz were not themselves demolished by the fleeing SS until November 1944 and, as late as March 1945, a new gas chamber was opened at Ravensbrück camp.

In the world in general, however, it was clear that the end of Nazism would come sooner rather than later; and although the subsequent peace would bring its own problems of rebuilding a shattered Europe, at least the monstrous threat to humanity which had hung over the world for more than five years would have been removed.

But as people in Britain opened their newspapers one morning in the late autumn of 1944, they read that their Resident Minister in the Middle East, Lord Moyne, an alumnus of Eton College and a hero of the First World War, had been assassinated in Cairo. It emerged later that he had been killed by members of the Stern Gang.

The general reaction in Britain was one of shock and dismay, but the reason for Moyne's violent death was not far to seek. His support for the Arabs was open, and in December 1941 he had requested the Turkish authorities to turn back a refugee ship, the *Struma*, despite the strongest appeals from Jewish Palestine. The *Struma* had subsequently foundered and sunk in the Black Sea with considerable loss of life. Then, in May 1944, Lord Moyne had received an emissary from Adolf Eichmann, the architect of the destruction of the Hungarian Jews and one of the principal administrators of the Final Solution. Eichmann's proposal was the exchange of one million Jews for lorries and equipment. Moyne's response was popularly reputed to have been: "What would I do with one million Jews?"

As the Second World War drew to its end and Jewish Palestine seemed no closer to achieving its principal aim of statehood, the Stern Gang – whose leader had been killed in 1942 – decided to step up its campaign to force the British out of Palestine all together. How far their tactics were successful is a matter of debate: they may have speeded the process up, for it is certain that the British, obstinate though they were, were also tired of mediating in the endless and unresolvable struggle between Arab and Jew.

Lord Moyne was an obvious target because he was an appointee of an elected government whose remit was to remain disinterested, but who nevertheless took an openly anti-Semitic stance. Once the decision had been made to kill him, two members of the Gang were selected to carry out the assassination. Eliahu Bet-Tsouri was twenty-three, fair-haired and fluent in Arabic. Dressed in a tweed jacket and smoking a pipe, he could easily pass for a young British officer wandering through Egypt on a few days' leave. His companion, Eliahu

Hakim, was dark-skinned and indistinguishable in appearance from a native Egyptian. He had already proved himself by running much-needed guns and ammunition back from Egypt to Palestine for the Stern Gang on many occasions.

Planning was obviously a vital part of such a major operation. Once in Cairo, the two members of the hit team joined forces with the Stern Gang's resident member in Egypt and studied the daily routine and habits of the British Minister with care. Once they were satisfied, they selected a date for the attempt: 6 November. They armed themselves and took up the positions they had chosen. It was just after 1 p.m. when Lord Moyne's car turned the corner where they were waiting and headed towards them. Moyne was seated in the back with his secretary. As the car pulled up outside the Residence, Hakim and Bet-Tsouri took aim; but the Minister's chauffeur saw them, leapt from the car and very bravely tried to disarm them. In the struggle one of the guns went off, fatally wounding Lord Moyne. The two members of the Stern Gang managed to get away on their bicycles in the confusion which followed, though a passing policeman gave chase on his motorbike. Hakim and Bet-Tsouri were under strict orders not to harm any Egyptian, though they did fire at their pursuer, without effect.

It was not long, however, before they were arrested and charged. The world's press thronged to the trial, along with representatives of Britain's CID and intelligence services, who hoped to learn more about the Jewish militant underground by attending.

The two men stood by their action. "We did what we had to do," said Bet-Tsouri, "and it was just. We do not fight for the preservation of the Balfour Declaration or for the National Home. We fight for freedom and the independence of our land of Israel."

Both men were sentenced to death. The established Jewish authorities in Palestine viewed Moyne's killing as a setback and feared British reprisals in one form or another. Chaim Weizmann was so appalled that he assured the British that the terrorist groups would be extirpated once and for all. The news of Moyne's death came to him, he said, as a shock as great as the news of his own son's death in the Battle of Britain.

Despite general revulsion at the attack, pleas for clemency for the two men came from abroad, and for a time it looked as if they might be pardoned. However, at the insistence of Winston Churchill, who was a close friend of Moyne's, no reprieve was granted, and in March 1945 both men were led to the gallows. They refused to be bound or blindfolded. They declared that they were not afraid to look death in the eye and, just before the order to release the trap was given, they began to sing the *Hatikvah*.

In 1975, the Egyptian Government agreed to return the embalmed bodies to Israel for reburial. Now, both men lie on Jerusalem's Mount Herzl. The bodies were handed over to Yitzhak Shamir, himself a former leader of the Stern Gang, at a ceremony on the Israeli–Egyptian border. Shamir was asked formally to identify the bodies of the two men:

> I recognised them at once. Their faces were untouched and calm. Neither time nor the way they had died had disfigured them. A chaplain told me that only the righteous are granted this privilege. I hope so and I believe that it is so. The Government of Israel was represented at their funeral, and I delivered the eulogy.

At the time, however, the Jewish leadership made an all-out attempt to clamp down on extremist nationalist organisations. If the British were angry at the assassination in Cairo, the Zionist leaders were furious. They believed that these acts of terror placed the Jewish community in great jeopardy, and they were determined that such atrocities should not occur again. They went so far as to declare that anyone found to be a member of any of the underground groups would be turned over to the British immediately.

Weizmann believed that the activities of such groups undermined the kind of Zionism he had advocated all his life. Since the beginning, both he and Ben-Gurion had worked to bring about a solution to the problems of Palestine by putting political pressure on Britain. And yet, to those who supported the Irgun and the Stern Gang, there seemed to be no other way to break the vicious circle of negotiation with an intractable Mandatory Power – which needed Arab oil and free passage through the Suez Canal – than by acts of violence.

As early as 1942, even Ben-Gurion was inclining towards the idea of putting pressure on Britain by at least using the threat of "uncontrollable" terrorism. The need for an independent Jewish state was given greater urgency by the discovery at the end of the war of the full horror of the concentration camps. The Allies had known about Auschwitz since 1943, and yet no attempt had been made to bomb either it or the railway lines which served it. Why not? This is a question which has still not been adequately answered.

It was no wonder that many Jews felt that the only way to vent their frustration was through violence; their patience with British rule was stretched to breaking point, and perhaps contained only by the limits of their own resources.

Chapter Fifteen:
In Search of Wealthy Friends

It was the height of summer, and New York was hot. Ben-Gurion set off, his white shirt open at the neck and his jacket thrown over one shoulder. He was glad that his friend's penthouse was within walking distance. Once more he was in the land of wealthy allies, of people who felt as strongly as he did that the British Mandate must end.

With him on this trip was the Treasurer of the Jewish Agency. They had taken rooms at the St Moritz Hotel, from which Ben-Gurion had telephoned his old friend Rudolf G. Sonneborn. This rich, Harvard-educated businessman had been a pilot in the First World War, and a strong supporter of Zionism since his youth. He had first met Ben-Gurion at the Paris Peace Conference of 1919–20. Both men were realists and knew that, although most Jews were prepared to fight for their homeland, the eternal question was: fight with what? They needed more arms and ammunition if they were to continue to show their resentment of the British military presence in Palestine.

Ben-Gurion was far from being a military man, yet he now saw clearly that, if the Jewish homeland was to be made secure, he needed to find the means with which Jews could defend themselves.

Sonneborn had given him directions over the telephone and assured his friend that he was anxious to see him again.

The American had invited seventeen others to the meeting on 1 July 1945 with Ben-Gurion and the Jewish Agency Treasurer. Once the introductions were over, they sat down and waited to hear what their distinguished visitor had to say. They listened intently as Ben-Gurion explained how their lives, and those of all Jews, were bound together by the fragile strip of desert land called Palestine. Each of them nodded in understanding. Palestine may have been 5,000 miles away but there was no question of their link with their ancestral homeland. Ben-Gurion spoke so softly that some of those present had to lean forward to catch his words; yet the power of his message filled the room.

The Nazis had slaughtered 11 million people in the camps, of whom nearly 6 million were Jews. The ancient Jewish communities of Europe had been all but destroyed. While it was true that many nations sympathised with the Jewish plight now, that sympathy would fade with the passage of time, and action had to be taken at once. Riots had started among the Jewish survivors of the Holocaust who now found themselves in displaced persons camps (known as DPs). Few still had families, even fewer had homes to which they could return. All they wanted was to get out of Europe and start a new life. Ben-Gurion had a simple question for those assembled in the room: would the USA take the refugees?

It might have been a simple question, but it was difficult to find an answer. Like everywhere else, the USA had a quota system. Homes could probably be found for those survivors with relatives already in the States who were willing to vouch for them; but relationships would have to be proved and most of the people in the DP camps had no papers any more. In any case, the number allowed into the USA would be relatively small.

Ben-Gurion suddenly spoke again, his soft voice cutting into the silence that had fallen in the room. There was one country which would take them. Palestine. And Palestine needed them. The Arab population was nearly twice as big as the Jewish, and yet the Jews had to reach a majority if they were ever really going to be able to call the country "home".

He paused and reached for a glass of water. As he drank, he studied the faces of the people around him. Had he convinced this influential group of businessmen and community leaders?

If the British left Palestine now, he continued, there would be
a power vacuum which would quickly be filled by the majority
group – the Arabs. In such a case, an Arab-Jewish war would be
inevitable, for the Jews would not let go of what they had fought
so hard to gain, and they would defend to the death what they
so desperately needed: a secure homeland at last, where no Jew
need fear discrimination or persecution.

And then Ben-Gurion made his final request. Years later,
Sonneborn would write:

> On that memorable day, we were asked to form ourselves into an
> American arm of the underground Haganah. We were given no clue
> as to what we might be called upon to accomplish, when the call
> might come, or who would call us. We were simply asked to be
> prepared and to mobilise like-minded Americans. We were asked to
> keep the meeting confidential.

This the group did, and no notes were taken of the discussions
they'd had.

Meanwhile, those who had survived the horrors of the war
were having to cope both with traumatic memories and the
demands of trying to survive further in a confused and still
violent world. Sam Bresler had watched as his mother and his
little sister had been dragged away by the SS to die in the gas
chambers:

> My father couldn't get to them. The day it happened was also my
> sister's sixth birthday. My father and I survived the war but only
> just. At the beginning of May 1945, the SS took us to a place near
> Hamburg. They told us that the war was almost over and that they
> were going to put us on a ship which would take us to Sweden to
> recuperate. She was the *Capricorna*, a liner which they'd converted
> into a troopship. We were loaded on and then had to climb down
> and down into the bowels of the ship. By the time we'd reached the
> tenth deck I said to my father, "I don't care where we're going, but
> I'm going back up."
>
> We got as far as the first deck. At about midday, a British plane
> flew over the harbour and the SS started shooting at it. So the plane
> dropped a couple of bombs. They didn't know the ship had about

8,000 survivors on it. She started to sink, and only 312 of us got out alive. The people on the lower decks were trapped. It was 3 May: less than a week before the end of the war.

Sam was anxious to get to Palestine as soon as possible:

The Warburg Bank family donated a home in British-occupied territory for 100 children who had survived the war. I went to school there for two years. After that, although I could have gone to Canada, I decided to go to Palestine. I wanted to pick up a gun. I wanted my self-respect back.

Sam subsequently joined the Haganah, and then the Palmach. The Haganah had become an underground organisation again after the war. Another kind of war, against the British, was beginning.

Within months of the end of the Second World War, legal Jewish immigration into Palestine came to an end. The last ship arrived in Haifa carrying 340 refugees from Barcelona. David Ben-Gurion, who had visited the sites of Bergen-Belsen and Dachau, and returned to Jerusalem a deeply shaken man, saw however a glimmer of hope in the change of government in Britain at the end of July 1945. He was to be sorely disappointed. The Labour Party had constantly espoused the Jewish cause while it was in opposition. Now, the new Labour Government, even in the face of the evidence which was emerging about the death camps, declared its support of the 1939 White Paper. They went further and stated that any illegal efforts by Jews to reach Palestine would be rigorously opposed. The British Mediterranean fleet was ordered to police all vessels bound for Palestine, and to turn back any carrying would-be settlers.

The Jews could not believe that they had been so heartlessly betrayed by a country with which they had fought a common enemy for six years. But as the reality sank in, they braced themselves once again to outwit and outmanoeuvre the forces of a nation which they now not only detested, but despised.

Chapter Sixteen: Breaking and Entering

During the war, the British set up detention camps on the island of Cyprus, which had been a British colony since 1925. The plan was to put all those would-be immigrants to Palestine into them until such time as there might be quota openings. This system continued and the camps were maintained after the war, and many Jews, having survived Nazi imprisoment, now found themselves once again behind barbed wire.

Ike Katz, having survived the war, made up her mind to go to Palestine. She didn't realise how difficult it would be, but at sixteen years old she had seen enough under the Nazis to steel her resolve despite anything life might throw at her:

> Having come back from the concentration camps, my entire age group, all of us, organised ourselves into Zionist youth clubs. Our main aim was to get to Palestine as soon as possible. I came home and told my mother that I had decided to go. To my mother's credit, sad as she was, she did not discourage me. So I went with her blessing. The idea of our own youth club was that once we got to Palestine, we would establish a kibbutz.
>
> For a long time it was touch and go. We had our bags packed days in advance, wondering whether we'd get a train at all. When one did arrive, we found that it was a goods train; but our entire bunch of thirty or forty people found space in one of the wagons.

It was bitterly cold, so we huddled together to try and keep warm. We were on the train for maybe fifteen hours.

Eventually we got to the Danube and took a boat to Bulgaria. The people there got another wagon on a goods train ready, with straw for us to lie down on. When we eventually reached Varna, there were two gigantic ships waiting. In each of the holds there were three or four levels of bunks like shelves, and we were packed into them like sardines – 8,000 of us in each ship. It was so crowded that if one person wanted to turn over, everyone else had to turn over at the same time. After a few hours we found it impossible to breathe, so we had to struggle up on to the decks for some air.

The food consisted of biscuits. The first day they were beautiful. On the second and third day they began to smell. You just couldn't eat them, but there was nothing else. On the third day, however, someone handed out cans of grapefruit juice from Palestine. Luckily, our group got hold of one of the cans. There was just enough juice for exactly one tablespoon per person. That is the most wonderful memory I have of the trip. We sailed down the Black Sea coast, through the Bosphorus, across the Sea of Marmara, and through the Dardanelles into the Mediterranean, where, lo and behold, six British destroyers appeared. They'd known all along about our two ships and all the "illegals" on board. They signalled our ships' captains and escorted us to Cyprus.

Eventually, Ike did get to Palestine, but travelling there was always hard, and only the most determined could make it successfully. Perhaps that in itself was not such a bad thing for the Jews. Hadassah Braun, born in Austria, had the right spirit for the journey. At the end of 1938, she fled with her parents to Krakow in Poland. When the Germans invaded in 1940, her father, with the help of a friend, was able to get hold of some forged documents; but soon afterwards her parents were arrested and taken to the camps, where they perished. In 1943, aged sixteen, Hadassah made her way across war-torn Europe to the little village where her father had lived as a boy, because he had told her that there was a priest there who would help her. She reached the village successfully, and the friendly priest, who had just been released from prison for sheltering Jews, directed her to the Hungarian border:

I had a map, but I couldn't read it and I very soon got lost. I wandered for three days before a German frontier guard found me. I stayed with the guards, washing their clothes and doing dishes, until an officer arrived and said that I would have to be deported. I escaped in the night and made my way through the mountains as a stowaway on a goods train.

I jumped off the train at a small village. It was pouring with rain so I went to a house and asked for shelter. It was the home of a priest, who was very nervous of helping me because I was a Jew; but a woman visitor said she would take me in, and I stayed with her until the Russian Army arrived.

Then I joined the Russians and worked for them as a laundrywoman. When they crossed the German border, they found that my German was better than that of their own interpreters, so I became an interpreter for them. I served in that capacity for almost nine months. Then I got a job with the Swiss Red Cross. It was a good way of getting food.

It was 1945 by now, of course. The only documents I had were forged ones with a false name – and I'd been using them for a year. Whole populations were on the move in Europe; but as the authorities took me for a Polish girl I was repatriated there. Luckily I still had Jewish friends in Krakow and I bumped into one of them on the street – she'd worked in my father's office before the war. She was astonished to see me alive still and asked me what my plans were and whether I intended to go away – to America, or to a kibbutz in Palestine, she asked. I didn't know what a kibbutz was, so I went and looked the word up. I still didn't quite understand, but an old family friend later introduced me to a group of young Jews who were planning to go to Palestine and actually *form* a kibbutz!

It was 1947 by then and I was twenty. I decided to join them. Some of them had survived the camps, others had lived through years of forced labour in Russia. There were about twenty-five of us to begin with, and our leader was already in contact with a kibbutz in Palestine which was helping him make the arrangements to get us there.

Everything happened very suddenly. One night we were told that we were to be smuggled into Czechoslovakia, and that we could only take a small rucksack with us. This was hard for me, because through all my adventures I had hung on to a set of books which were a last memento of my parents. Now, I wouldn't be able to take them.

We set off in a train which stopped at the border where a uniformed guard told us to get down with our bags. He guided us through a small village and I remember asking whether we had passed the frontier yet. We crossed Czechoslovakia, and then Austria. In Vienna we were put up in a big encampment, living in a large overcrowded hall for six months. There, I met a boy from my old school. We talked together all night.

Eventually we were smuggled into Italy. We crossed the Brenner Pass on foot: it took the entire night – eleven hours. Then we travelled south to Verona. Of course we complained bitterly during the tough parts of the journey, but we never lost sight of our aim, or lost any of our determination to achieve it. Still, you must remember that all of us had suffered terrible hardships during the war, and, most importantly of all, we were all lonely. We were all sole survivors of families.

In Verona, someone was supposed to make contact with us, but he wasn't there, though we stayed at the railway station as we'd been told and waited for him. We'd also been told that if anyone asked us who we were and what we were doing there, we were to tell them that we were Greeks on the way home. None of us spoke Greek; but eventually the stationmaster came up and questioned us in German. I simply told him that we were waiting for someone. But then we noticed a police car parked not far away, and that made us nervous, so I told the stationmaster our cover story. "Greeks returning to Greece, eh?" he said, laughing. "And I don't suppose you have any papers?" I told him that the person we were waiting for had the papers. "OK," he answered. "You have no railway tickets and no documents. I think this is a matter for the police."

We were terribly tired after the trip we had made, and we were ready to give ourselves up, when suddenly one of our group, Lorna, who was younger than I was and a survivor of Auschwitz, stepped forward and rolled up her sleeve. "If you want to see a document, here is one," she said. "A number." He looked at the number tattooed on her arm and was moved. "How old are you?" he asked, and she said, "Sixteen." And he said, "And you were a child in a concentration camp?" And she said, "Yes; and now I suppose I'm going to be arrested for it."

He looked at her for a moment. "Not if I have anything to do with it. Where would you like to go?" We told him that we had

better get to the refugee centre in Milan. And he put us on a train
for Milan.

Much later, when we had sorted our further travel arrangements
out and re-established contact with Zionist Aliyah organisers, we
found ourselves in Genoa, where we slept in the corridor of a house
full of people like us. We were there for five months, waiting for a
ship to smuggle us to Palestine, but it was such a wonderful feeling to
have someone to take care of us. One day, almost without warning,
we were told we were about to leave. When we saw our ship, we
couldn't believe that this was the *actual* ship which would take us
to Palestine: we thought it was just a ferry to the "real" ship. It
was a freighter. It had an Israeli name which translated into English
meant "the survivors will return".

It was packed. There were four or five other groups like ours, and
seven layers of "shelves" for us to bunk down on. We were squashed
in like sardines and we spent twenty-one days at sea – during which
time one of the girls gave birth. She'd kept her pregnancy secret because
she wouldn't have been allowed on board in her condition. Someone
who'd done a week's first-aid course delivered the baby. The Italian
captain of the ship, a man of seventy-odd, coped with the event with
great sangfroid.

The main problem on the ship was the lack of water. In the last few
days of the voyage we ran out completely. But by then we had heard
the aeroplanes, and we knew we'd been spotted. Soon afterwards
we woke up to find two large British ships standing off us. Their
sides overshadowed us. Even so we decided to put up a fight; but
they responded with tear gas. Tear gas is a terrible thing: when you
breathe it in, you really think you are going to die.

We were escorted into the harbour at Haifa and transferred to a
ship for Cyprus, where they detained us for nearly a year.

The British were faced with a very difficult choice. Turning
away the refugees made them seem like heartless brutes; but
if they allowed them into Palestine, they risked an increase in
Arab unrest. The riots of 1939 were still a fresh memory despite
the war, and then there had been 1,350 casualties and 300 killed.
Now, it could be much worse. Then, however, three illegal ships
had been sent back to their Danube ports. Increased pressure at
home meant that at least now immigrants would not be sent

back to Europe. Keeping them in Cyprus was an expensive business, but the British did their best to make things there as comfortable as possible, as Hadassah Braun remembers:

The conditions in Cyprus were not bad. We didn't starve. The food wasn't good, but it was at least food. We were able to follow events in Palestine, and people came from there to give us Hebrew lessons.

We lived in a corrugated iron hut, in what had probably once been a military camp. I shared a small room with one other person. It was terribly hot in the summer, but for those who'd been in the *Konzentrationslager*, the worst thing was the sense of being imprisoned in a camp again.

One early spring day, however, the British decided to free people from Cyprus who were under seventeen years old. I was twenty-one, but since I looked much younger my group decided that I should go with them. They had already prepared some false birth certificates.

We left with a big British ship and were taken to Haifa. We were preparing to disembark when a small boat came out to the ship and the men on board told our captain that the port was sealed off owing to a shooting incident involving Arabs. The captain was far from happy, but he sailed south to Tel Aviv where a flotilla of little boats came out to ferry us ashore: these were manned by the people of the town who'd heard we were coming and spontaneously organised themselves to meet us.

I spent my first night in Tel Aviv in the small basement flat of a harbour porter. People were taking us in where they could. The next day the Jewish Agency made arrangements for me to go to a refugee camp, where I spent three days sharing a tent with a Moroccan family who became my friends for life. As soon as I could sort it out, I left for a kibbutz with three other girls. When I got there, I spent the first night since before the war in a bed with sheets – almost ten years!

I worked in the kibbutz for three months before I was mobilised. The kibbutz was wrong for us since it was full of older people – in their thirties, with families. I was in Haifa on the day independence was declared. I thought of my parents then. I hadn't wanted to leave them. My father was a communist and my mother was a Zionist. They were both fighters. My mother said to me, "Go. Maybe you will survive. Then you will be there when the Jews get their state, an independent state; and you will see what kind of state it will be."

Although pressure from the USA and the international Jewish community persuaded Britain to allow limited immigration after all in the years immediately following 1945, the British could not yet be moved to increase the quotas. They would, however, soon discover that no wall was high enough to deter Jews who were prepared to risk their very lives in order to reach the Promised Land.

Chapter Seventeen: Struggling in the Net

Shortly after the war, the US President, Harry Truman, suggested to Britain that it might allow 100,000 Jewish refugees into Palestine as a humanitarian gesture. Britain refused, but, weakened by the war and under constant pressure in Palestine itself from Jews and Arabs alike, made a counter-suggestion that the USA might be interested in helping to solve the problem of immigration. As a result, an Anglo-American Committee of Inquiry was set up in November 1945, which visited DP camps in Europe and interviewed the leaders of British and US Jewry. The Committee started its investigations in Palestine early in spring 1946.

One of those who appeared before it was the future Israeli premier, Golda Meir. "We only want that which is naturally given to all peoples of the world," she told them. "To be masters of our own fate ... to have the chance to bring the surviving Jewish children, of whom not so many are left in the world now, to this country, so that they may grow up like other youngsters who were born here, free of fear, with heads held high ..."

But it was difficult to know whether or not the members of the Committee could empathise with the feelings of the Jewish people for Palestine; and as they continued their investigation the Royal Navy equally continued to turn illegal refugee ships back.

Those who managed to make landfall and were identified by the authorities were counted and their number subtracted from the monthly quota. What the British never quite understood, however, was that they were dealing with people whose only future lay in Palestine – people whose history, both personal and public, had been wrecked in Europe; people who had nothing to lose.

Jews who had escaped the horror of the concentration camps and managed to avoid the Nazi fury by going into hiding were nevertheless scarred by the experience. Laura Leven had spent the war hiding in an underground bunker with no light and little air. Now, aged fourteen, she was free and ready to fulfil her dream of getting to Palestine:

The journey itself was fantastic. Everything was organised by the Zionist Youth Movement. We left Czechoslovakia illegally, using false names, and made our way to Belgium, where we stayed for nine months. Then we travelled right across Europe to Marseilles and spent a night in a field outside the town before boarding our ship the next morning.

We were on board for two weeks, 2,700 of us crammed together on shelves about twenty inches wide. The captain was a member of the Haganah but he wore civilian clothes; he was only twenty. Unfortunately we were seen by British spotter planes, so we knew that the Navy would intercept us. When they finally caught up with us, the captain came and hid among us. The other undercover members of the Haganah on board told us what would happen next, so we were prepared.

We weren't too far from Haifa, so we decided to make a run for it. The Haganah told us to throw tin cans at the British and fight them off as best we could if they tried to come alongside. We were just outside Haifa when they started shooting. They captured our ship in the middle of the night. The sea was calm and it was very dark, when suddenly there was bright light everywhere from their searchlights. The British captain shouted to us over a loud-hailer that we were in British waters and that we were to surrender. We yelled back, "No!" and started singing the *Hatikvah*. They fired over our heads and aimed water cannon at us. We didn't stand a chance.

Then they took us to Cyprus, where we spent nine months.

Werner Braun, his wife and his mentally disabled daughter lived underground with a succession of friends in Denmark for four years. In the end he used his savings to pay a fisherman to take them to Sweden:

> We left for Palestine in 1946. By then I had some more money saved and I even had a motorbike, which I was able to take with me. We arrived at our destination with no trouble and after I'd got the bike off the ship, we drove off the dock, all three of us clinging to one another. I might think twice about doing that again!

Professor Marge Landsberg had also spent the war in hiding with her family. Her home town in Holland was liberated by the Jewish Brigade:

> It was wonderful to see the Star of David on their uniforms. My father was so excited that he rushed out into the street and dragged some of them into our house and offered them food. I got to know one of them well later on. I liked him very much and, as I didn't want to live in Holland any longer, I accepted his proposal of marriage and agreed to follow him to Palestine. As he was officially a British soldier and I was his bride, I would have the "honour" of being taken to Palestine in a British troop ship. He had gone on ahead to Palestine where he was already settled, but we had to wait months to follow – there were several other women in the same situation as I was. First of all we were taken to England, where I refused to have anything to do with the ordinary British soldiers, whom I regarded as the enemy because of what was happening in Palestine. At last we set sail from Southampton. It was a long, unpleasant voyage.
>
> We docked at Haifa and our first experience of Palestine was an extremely rude reception by an Arab woman customs officer! My husband was waiting for me and he had found somewhere to live – in the laundry-room of a small hotel! We had no money and nothing to eat. I couldn't speak Hebrew either. The following day I managed to get a job in a florist's, and, as many of the customers were Arabs, I soon picked up some Arabic. I also discovered that in the Middle East people haggle, which was a new experience for me. At first it quite upset me, and of course I didn't really like the work – though I knew I was lucky to have found anything at all.

The things that struck me first were the bright light, the hot sun and the deep blue of the sky. The easy-going way of life was new, too. People wore shorts and casual clothes, and simply dropped in on one another all the time – there were no telephones, anyway!

Our baby was born just before the War of Independence started. Haifa was bombed and I remember running out of our house with my baby in my arms because of the sirens. My husband was in the war and he was the only survivor of a group that was attacked by the Arab Legion.

The marriage didn't last. I think the pressures of the new environment were just too hard. I was young and inexperienced then, and things were quite simply too tough.

Ike Katz remembers very well the day she finally reached Palestine after her release from Cyprus:

We were taken from the port in armoured cars. We travelled through Arab villages and in each one there was shooting. Finally we reached a transit camp where all sorts of paperwork was done. We stayed there three days.

Then our entire group – fifty or sixty of us – was taken to an institute called Ganja House, where we began a crash course. In a year's worth of evening classes we learnt all about Jewish history, and the Hebrew language. Normally it would take four years at university to assimilate the knowledge they crammed into us then. One teacher was especially good: she really radiated the spirit of Zionism.

As well as working in the fields by day and studying by night, we were divided into groups of ten soon after our arrival for military training. This lasted for two weeks, in which we were taught to shoot and to march. They made us into instant soldiers.

Very early on, in the April that I was there, the Haganah launched an attack on an Arab village in Galilee, in retaliation for an attack the villagers had made on one of our settlements. The settlement was a special one, it was the one where Ben-Gurion had spent his youth; so we had to make an example of the Arabs. The Haganah mobilised local forces for the job and we had to contribute ten people for the action. I was one of them. I'd only been in the country a month and already I was a soldier on active service! My Hebrew was still very bad and I had to ask people to say things twice before I could understand.

The plan was to travel as far as Tiberias by lorry and from there march the remaining six or seven kilometres overnight, to launch our attack at dawn. When the shooting started, I became bewildered and I began to cry. It wasn't that I was scared; I just didn't know who was shooting at what.

A richer and more fortunate immigrant, this time from South Africa, was Percy Manham:

We travelled on a cargo ship. She'd only take a maximum of twelve people – otherwise they'd've had to have a doctor on board. As soon as she left port, the whole family succumbed to seasickness. But we made it through the voyage all right, and got to the homeland without incident. There, I was surprised at first to see Jews doing all the kinds of menial jobs, like roadsweeping, which I was used to seeing Blacks do back in SA. But fairly soon I became accustomed to seeing bearded Hasidim on three-wheeler delivery bikes!

We found a house through an estate agent and Granny and I went to give it the once-over. It was on a sandy street that hadn't been developed much yet. The house itself was sparsely furnished but it had chandeliers and nice velvet curtains. We agreed to take it. The owner was very pleased to hear that I was from South Africa – South Africans had a very good reputation in Palestine – but she wanted two years' rent in advance and an undertaking that I would vacate the house at the end of that time. I had to close the deal quickly because she was leaving for the States the following Sunday; but I managed it.

I'd been told to buy a few sticks of furniture immediately, as an unfurnished place was an invitation to squatters. I remember going round the shops frantically buying this and that before they closed one Friday afternoon. And so we settled in; but a little later on a taxi-driver told me that the previous tenant had run the place as a brothel. Granny was horrified and got the maid to clean the bathroom and lavatory not once, but twice!

The situation in Palestine was deteriorating fast, with unrest spreading at an alarming rate. Unable to control the situation in any other way, the British authorities clamped down hard on the Jewish population. Some 100,000 troops and nearly 2,000 policemen raided dozens of villages and kibbutzim. The offices of the Jewish Agency were searched, and a curfew was imposed on all cities with a Jewish population. More than 3,000 people were summarily imprisoned in an attempt to force the Jews to toe the British line; but the attempt failed miserably. The Jews were doggedly determined to ride out every storm.

Channa Levi came to Palestine from New York. She had just finished High School and had decided to go to Palestine in 1947 after two weeks at an upstate youth camp:

That's where things really sparked, because it was completely Zionist. There was a group of Palestinians there and we soaked up everything they had to tell us about the country. One of my room-mates told me about a work study plan which took you to Palestine for a year, and I applied for it. Only fifteen girls from the whole of the USA were selected to go, but I was one of them! It was tough persuading my father to let me go, but he relented in the end. It was sad to say goodbye to everyone, but my brother, who was a professional photographer, took a great family portrait of us all just before I boarded the ship for the Middle East.

The accommodation on board was pretty awful – it was a converted troopship and I shared a cabin with twenty other women. I'd got an upper bunk. My mother, who'd travelled steerage to the United States, had advised me never to take a lower bunk in case the person above you threw up! There were lots of Arab women on board, bound for Beirut; below me was a mother with two small children, whose husband was in the male quarters in another part of the ship. The only person I knew at all was a girl I'd never met before, though we'd corresponded. We're friends to this day.

It was a long crossing, but when we finally arrived the British had closed the customs office for the night, so we had to stay on board until they reopened the next morning. I remember the tremendous searchlights they had, which swept the harbour to pick up illegal boats. It was a beautiful night and we could see bonfires being lit on the mountain behind the port. It seemed as if they were being lit just for us.

Meanwhile, illegal immigration was continuing, not only by sea, but across land borders. There, members of the Palmach frequently acted as guides. Hayim Hefer was one of them:

Our job was to smuggle people in across the borders with Syria and Lebanon. Naturally, we had agents in those countries who'd send us radio messages to let us know when a group of illegal immigrants was on its way. In Damascus, we had a bunch of women agents who used teaching work as their cover. Our girls had a flat next door to the British Embassy. I remember that when they needed somewhere high up for their radio antenna, they managed to rig it to the flagpole on the roof of the embassy!

I did the job for a year, and it was one of the happiest times of my life. But it was dangerous. One night after it had been raining hard we were ankle-deep in mud as we made our way to meet a lorryload of immigrants. As I helped the first ones out, I saw that they were a mother with a girl of nine and two twins of about three. Little children were always a problem because they were apt to cry, and when they did it was as bad as ringing a bell in all that quiet, open country. So, I always used to carry some wine, sugar and coffee in my rucksack. I gave the twins a little wine and sugar each to make them sleepy, and carried one of them while the mother carried the other.

We began to pick our way across the frontier through the mud and I could see that the little girl was having a hard time. She could speak some Hebrew because she'd learnt it at the *shul* in Damascus. "If you throw away your shoes, you'll find it easier," I told her. "We'll get you some new ones when you get to your kibbutz." She looked at me sternly and said, "I bought these shoes specially to set foot on the soil of Palestine for the first time." I was so moved that I just stood there in the dark. "All right," I said, "give me your shoes and I'll put them in my rucksack. You can put them on again when we reach the border."

Unfortunately soon after that one of the twins began to cry. The commander of our group told me to stay behind with the little family for fear that as we crossed over into Palestine the noise would be heard in the Arab villages nearby, and they would raise the alarm. But it was too late anyway. Suddenly there was firing all around us: we'd stumbled into a British border patrol. We returned fire, but after a few rounds our guns jammed. We'd got them from a kibbutz in the north which had plenty of weapons but was a bit stingy about giving them away, so our stuff was old – from the First World War.

I hid the mother and children behind a rock. Our orders were to run. If the British arrested the family, the most they'd face was three weeks' detention. For us it would be nearer three years' jail. I put my coat round the little girl to keep her warm, and left them.

Later on, I found out that the little girl had cut my name out of the coat in case the British could trace me through it. They only kept the family prisoner for two weeks, then they let them go. I would have liked to have made contact with them again, but I wasn't able to trace them.

During this time of ferment, Ben-Gurion tirelessly travelled the country, showing that despite the danger he was there, ready to fight shoulder-to-shoulder with his people. One day, as Sam Bresler looked down from the watchtower by the stockade which surrounded his kibbutz, he saw a car approach and realised that Ben-Gurion was coming. Sam was so keen to meet him that once Ben-Gurion was inside the compound, he deliberately sounded the alarm, so that he could come down and "shelter" in the dugout where his hero had taken refuge!

The British continued their crackdown on Jewish rebellion. The leaders of the Haganah went into hiding. British searches for arms caches resulted in damage to property which further angered the Jewish community, and all the time the hatred and the tension mounted. Rita Bresler joined the underground through a friend who worked as an announcer for the illegal Jewish radio station. Her group were taught combat techniques using any weapon that came to hand. There were very few guns, and "we had to be able to take care of ourselves with anything, from a stone to a table-leg".

The anger they already felt was to be heightened by the events that occurred during the summer of 1946.

Chapter Eighteen: Fighting Back

The Anglo-American Committee of Enquiry published its report on 1 May 1946. It recommended that the immigration quotas and land purchase restrictions laid out in the White Paper of 1939 be rescinded. While President Truman broadly welcomed its findings (the report recommended the immediate admission of 100,000 immigrants), the Arab reaction was predictably hostile and the British Prime Minister, Clement Attlee, remarked frostily that the report would have to be "considered as a whole in all its implications". Not long afterwards the British said that they would not implement the report's recommendations unless the USA shared the cost. In June the Foreign Secretary, Ernest Bevin, told the Labour Party conference that the reason the Americans supported Jewish immigration to Palestine was that they didn't want "too many of them [i.e. Jews] in New York". In the same month the government authorised the High Commissioner in Palestine, Sir Alan Cunningham, to launch a security offensive against the Jewish Agency and the Haganah. The British action started on 29 June, promptly dubbed by the Jews "Black Saturday".

Four days earlier, David Shenhabi got word that he was on the British wanted list. He began to plan his means of escape. But whom should he turn to?

Where does a boy run when he is in trouble? To his parents, of course! I made my way home to Tel Aviv. That was on the Monday, and the town was under curfew. British paratroops were going from building to building, checking up on people.

I got to my parents' place but almost as soon as I'd arrived, on the Tuesday morning, somebody knocked at the door; I went and hid in another room as my mother opened it. There was a man in overalls, carrying a milk churn. She let him in and closed the door behind him. He said that he was from a kibbutz out of town and that he'd been given orders to get me away from Tel Aviv. In the churn was a set of overalls for me.

I then had to take the churn and wait for a lorry which would be sent to pick me up. It took me to a safe house where I spent four days before being taken to the Haganah HQ for southern Palestine. There, they told me that I was not going back to my kibbutz; they were putting me in charge of training for a large area of the country. It was very challenging work, and it carried a bonus with it: while I was running the training programme, I met my future wife!

At about the same time, Hayim Hefer got the news that Yitzhak Rabin had been arrested:

The British knew quite a lot about the Palmach's activities – they had a good intelligence network and plenty of informers. Rabin had broken his leg, so he couldn't get away.

We made plans immediately to get him out, and we managed to smuggle maps, a two-way radio and wire-cutters into the prison; but two days before we were set to go, the British released him.

Since we had everything prepared, we decided to go ahead anyway, and try to get as many of our people out as possible. The Haganah had concocted some home-made tear-gas bombs and I managed to smuggle one in with two policemen we'd bribed. The idea was that on the day of the break, our people inside would throw the bomb against the wall and create a diversion. We told them to rub lemon juice around their eyes to protect them from the effects of the tear-gas.

The whole thing turned out to be a disaster. They threw the bomb all right, but it didn't go off; and the lemon juice got into their eyes and half blinded them. Later on I got a letter from one of them:

"Dear Hayim, Next time you have any bright ideas, why not try them out on yourself first?!"

Ben-Gurion, who had escaped arrest during the full tide of the British military crackdown because he was abroad at the time, was furious at what he saw as an unprovoked attack on his people; but the British, and the military in particular, were getting increasingly impatient at the albatross of Palestine which hung round their neck. They were chary of offending the Arabs; but very few of them had much sympathy for the Jews. The crackdown was unsuccessful, and not only that but counter-productive, in that it served merely to provoke greater acts of violence from Jewish extremists.

The British had offices in the King David Hotel, and on 22 July 1946, the Irgun blew them up. The entire south-western corner of the hotel was destroyed, and victims were buried under a huge pile of debris. British troops and police sweated under the hot sun to bring out the wounded and the dead, and trails of blood marked the route of the stretcher-bearers. Ninety-one people died – Jews, Arabs and Britons – and a further seventy-odd were injured.

Lewis Harris was still serving in the British Army at that time. By now he was a staff captain, and he had left the King David five minutes before the bomb went off. He had had a lucky escape; but his loyalty to the British was not to be rewarded. Although he rose to the rank of major . . .

. . . in February 1947 my wife and I were asked to leave. As a "troublesome element" we were, in effect, thrown out. We came back to England but I was finished with the Army, and as soon as we were able we returned to Palestine. I got our permits from the Jewish Head of Immigration, who was a friend of the family. Now I was one of "us", rather than one of "them".

The bombing of the King David Hotel, although the Jewish Agency tried to justify it, did nothing for the Jewish cause in Palestine. Attlee had already remarked in private that "Jews must not try to get to the head of the queue"; and the GOC in Palestine, General Sir Evelyn Barker, who had commanded the troops who liberated Bergen-Belsen, when commenting on a military boycott of the Jewish community, said that the measures would "be punishing the Jews in a way the race dislikes as much as any, by striking at their pockets and showing our contempt for them". The Holocaust, at the time still little known and little understood, had not affected prevailing anti-Semitic sentiments much; and Jewish terrorism and Ben-Gurion's on/off dalliance with it did nothing to encourage sympathy in people who were predisposed to dislike and distrust the Jews in any case.

Crises among the would-be immigrants continued to occur. Back in April 1946 two Haganah ships carrying 1,014 people between them were preparing to leave the port of La Spezia in Italy when the Italians, under pressure from Britain, suddenly withdrew permission for them to sail. The desperate men, women and children on board refused to disembark, and mounted a hunger strike to draw the world's attention to their plight. If force was used against them, they declared, they would sink the ship and kill themselves.

Determined to show their support for the La Spezia Jews, the Jewish National Council decided to join in the hunger strike. Beds were set up in their Jerusalem offices and everyone taking part prepared to begin the fast. The only sustenance allowed was sugarless tea.

One problem was that on the third day of the strike, Passover would occur. The Chief Rabbi, Isaac Halevi Herzog, was insistent: according to Jewish law, all Jews must eat at the Passover Seder. Following a hastily called meeting, it was agreed that each participant in the strike would eat no more than a piece of matzah. Once agreed, they continued with their strike. News of their defiance had spread and crowds gathered outside, shouting encouragement.

Golda Meir was among the participants, but just before the strike was due to begin she made a last appeal to the authorities to allow the ships in La Spezia to sail. The British Chief Secretary asked her if she thought that His Majesty's Government was really going to change its policies just because she was refusing to eat; to which she replied, "No, I have no such illusions. If the deaths of six million Jews didn't change government policy, I don't expect that my not eating will do so."

But she was wrong. On 8 May, the two ships were at last given permission to sail to Palestine and the number of immigrants was deducted from the month's quota.

Miriam Spielman used the trick of arriving on a visit but staying permanently to circumvent the quota. She'd been living in England for nine years when she won a prize which gave her the opportunity to go on a trip to Palestine:

> I'd dreamt of going there for years. At the time in England I was working for a family as nanny to their little girl, who was three years old. I did everything for her; her mother was a very busy academic who didn't have much time for her. It wasn't until I was about to go that I realised how attached I'd become to the little girl; and it was traumatic for the child when I left, so it was a hard parting.
>
> We sailed from Southampton and we had to sign an undertaking for the organisers of the trip that we would return to England. Of course I signed, even though I had no intention of going back. It was the first dishonest act of my life!
>
> I felt very guilty after we had docked at Haifa; but stepping ashore was an overwhelming experience. To be in a country that belonged to the Jews! My sister was already living there and I stayed with her at first, but I had to make my own way sooner or later and I felt that I had to formalise somehow the fact that I was there at all. I went to see a man at the Jewish Agency who said, "Look, if you came here to settle, just disappear into the countryside – join one of the kibbutzim."
>
> The English rabbi in charge of the trip was furious when he found out that I intended to stay. Even though my brother-in-law had got me a doctor's letter to say that I was too ill to travel, he came to visit me at my sister's flat and gave me a terrible dressing-down. He banged my sister's glass table-top so hard I thought he would break it. He told me that he took my behaviour as a personal stain on his honour, but I also learnt that one of the other people on the trip had decided to stay too. I was very upset, but I stood my ground. I didn't see the rabbi again for some years, when I bumped into him in the street: it turned out that he, too, had decided to stay!

It was not only from Europe that Jews were arriving. Sara Tsuberi came from the Yemen in the early days:

We fled from Sa'na. It still wasn't permitted for Jews to leave for Palestine in those days. The king wouldn't let us leave; but we sold some of our things and made it look as if we were just going out for the day. The Yemenis treated the Jews like dogs; it was no place to stay.

We packed what we needed on to a donkey and made our way to Aden. The donkey didn't belong to us – Jews didn't own donkeys and we were very poor anyway – but we were able to hire it from an Arab neighbour. It was a hard journey and when we got to Aden we found Jews there who'd been waiting a year for the opportunity to get away. There was a lottery system to decide who would get a place on a ship. It was a matter of pure luck. We settled down in Aden to wait with everyone else and my sister and I found work as nannies. Eventually my parents' names came up and so did my sister's, but not mine, so they left without me. I wept and wept to see them go; but a month later my turn came and I followed them.

The Yemeni immigrants – nearly all, like Sara, desperately poor and uneducated – settled in Rosh Ha 'Ayin near Petach Tikvah. Here, a paediatrician called George Mundel, originally from South Africa, was attempting to establish a hospital with the help of Hadassah – the women's Zionist organisation of America:

I was the first doctor to arrive. The hospital consisted of several Nissen huts. There was no glass in the windows, no running water and no lavatories. There were several wards, but their distribution was confusing. When I arrived there were fourteen very small, dehydrated and undernourished babies in a room next to the kitchen, which was next to the soiled linen room. I found that they carried the soiled linen through the kitchen. We had to roll up our sleeves!

The two nurses I had sent an urgent message to Hadassah headquarters in Jerusalem. Soon, a couple of other paediatricians arrived and we set about organising the hospital. We reorganised the rooms, had window-panes put in, and eventually got sewage lines rather than the deep-pit latrines we had to be content with at the beginning. Then we got a laboratory complete with a technician, and an X-ray machine and a radiographer. In time, we had a 100-bed hospital up and running, but it still wasn't enough.

Much later, in 1948, we received lots of very sick children who'd come off the aeroplanes which flew Yemeni Jews in en masse during Operation Magic Carpet. They'd arrive at ten or eleven at night. Usually they were dehydrated and they had diarrhoea and high temperatures. Nearly all of them had malaria and many were suffering from typhoid, pneumonia or TB. About twenty children arrived every night and the camp around the hospital grew and grew. At one point I think there were about 17,000 people there. The people who worked in the camp and in the kitchens were new immigrants, too, but they came from eastern Europe and cooked Polish-style food, which the Yemenis shunned, preferring to cook for themselves.

Physical conditions weren't easy, either. I remember we had a plague of fieldmice. The whole place was invaded by them. You'd take your jacket off and when you put it back on, mice would jump out of the pockets. You'd even find mice in your briefcase!

But slowly we fixed the place up, and in the end we even had curtains on the windows. I recall that one day Rebecca Shulman, the President of Hadassah, came to visit us. We very proudly showed her that we had one room for very small babies which was all glassed in and had curtains and everything. We showed her what we were doing and how nice and clean everything was, but then suddenly Mrs Shulman stopped dead. "What's the matter?" we asked; and then we saw an enormous rat crawling out of the ceiling and down a curtain towards the children. Our administrator, a man called Schatz, caught the rat in the curtain, and took a pair of scissors and cut the curtain off!

We had a very high mortality rate. Many of the children had more than one disease, and they had no immunity. Over a weekend we'd typically have four or five deaths. And then there was polio. The first cases in Israel's polio epidemic occurred in Rosh Ha 'Ayin. I'd seen it before in Africa. This was truly infantile paralysis. I filled in the forms for infectious diseases and mailed them off to Jerusalem. Two weeks later a group from the Health Ministry came to see us. "What are you doing about the polio?" I asked them. "What polio?" they answered. "I sent you a notice about two weeks ago," I said. They replied, "Oh, we don't read our mail; why didn't you send a telegram?" Anyway, a big panic started and we began to get more and more cases, all over the country. Polio was endemic in Israel, and the Yemenis had no immunity to the disease. Eighty per cent of our victims were under three years old.

In addition to coping with that, we had to contend with the Yemenis in general, who were very suspicious of treatment. They would come and steal their babies out of the hospital. I remember that one child was stolen with an intravenous drip attached to him. Next morning the father returned the equipment but not the child. The child was very ill. I don't know if he survived.

Meanwhile the women were giving birth in terrible conditions. In the rainy season it was cold and muddy in the camp; but when the Health Ministry turned an old aircraft hangar into a vast nursery, there was a huge amount of cross-infection. Eventually the Women's International Zionist Organisation established a proper nursery in one of the Nissen huts, and we were able to save a lot of the children who came to us. I think the first Hebrew I really learnt was "Stop penicillin, start streptomycin"! Sometimes you'd see a child who looked past help and yet he would recover.

We gave transfusions too. I remember going to the blood bank in Tel Aviv where they kept the stuff in the fridges in ketchup bottles. We'd pour the blood into a burette and then strain it through gauze. No one would dream of doing that today!'

Dr Mundel's struggles to save infant lives in the new state are an indication of how much work there was still to be done even after independence had been achieved; but in 1946 independence still seemed to be nothing more than a distant dream. The British remained inflexible; the Arabs remained in the majority and commanded British sympathy. It is hard now to see why Britain did not show a greater sense of detachment. In the end, the fact that the USA, for example, took a pro-Jewish stance did not affect its trade relations with Arab states – at least in the first post-war decades, and even later, only such Muslim republics as Iran and Libya would declare open enmity.

In 1946, even though the King David Hotel bombing had clearly damaged the Jewish position, attacks on the British continued immediately. These were provoked by Britain's refusal to extend the Mandate under a United Nations trusteeship. Both the Haganah and the Stern Gang now began a series of attacks on the railways. Bridges and railway workshops were also targeted, but these attacks, though effective, were not without losses – the Sternists lost eleven men in the course of this campaign.

In return, the British again mobilised 100,000 troops and 1,500 police. Sir Evelyn Barker declared that he would hang a terrorist from every lamp-post in Palestine. A large number of Jewish leaders were detained and raids on the kibbutzim resulted in further arrests. The stepping up of action by the Irgun and the Stern Gang led, however, to a final split with the Haganah. The latter organisation had long been unhappy with its association with the extremists – it had not been formed to commit acts of violence against innocent people. It would continue to exist, but only as an organisation dealing with illegal immigration.

At the end of July 1946 a curfew was imposed on Tel Aviv. It lasted for four days while the military conducted house-to-house searches, hauling suspects off to the police stations for interrogation. Although the city was sealed tight, Yitzhak Shamir, by now the most important member of the Stern Gang, still felt confident that he could get through the British net. As I talked to him, he leaned back in his chair behind his oversized desk and smiled reminiscently:

> It's true. I felt very sure that I could make it. I'd attended a meeting with my wife just before the curfew was imposed and we'd lost track of time. Even when I realised that we'd missed the deadline to get out I wasn't particularly disturbed. I always thought that if I was ever trapped I could dress up as a devout Jew with a black coat and a false beard. Unfortunately, though, the CID had been tipped off and they'd surrounded the house. They shouted for me to come out, and, of course, I did.

After a couple of weeks in solitary confinement, in mid-August Shamir was taken from his cell, hand-cuffed, driven to the airport and flown in a Halifax bomber into exile in Eritrea.

Chapter Nineteen: New Blood

Ben-Gurion's continuing fight to achieve his dream had the support of most of the Jews in the Diaspora. For those young enough to be without roots or commitments in their native countries, the lure of Palestine was great. Leslie Read's family were English Zionists; when Leslie felt that the time had come to join the fight, he didn't hesitate:

> I decided that I wanted to try and help in some way, if they would accept me. I felt like a secret agent. In Manchester I was given an address to go to in London, and there I was given an address in Paris. When I reported to the Parisian address, they sent me on to Marseilles. There, they stuck me in the back of a lorry and drove me to a camp outside the town called G.
>
> I was there for two or three weeks before I was suddenly told that I would be going to Israel that very night. I was only allowed to take one smallish bag. My travelling companions and I were taken to Marseilles Airport at some time after midnight, and after customs we boarded a DC3 – which I remember looked a bit dodgy; in fact I'm convinced that parts of it were held together with string. Anyway, it took off and soon we were flying over the Mediterranean. We landed in a field outside Haifa. We all piled out and the plane took off again immediately. They'd taken my British passport away from me in France – it was stamped "not valid for travel to Palestine" – and

given me some documents which I couldn't read but which I gathered said that I was a displaced person permitted to travel to Palestine.

It felt a bit odd, standing in the middle of a field in what seemed like the middle of nowhere in the middle of the night, with papers that I couldn't read and no way of getting back.

Ben Ocopnick, from Canada, had a similar urge to join the fight for independence; but he didn't want to let on to his parents:

Of course I didn't tell my parents that I was going to fight. I told them I was going to do some work in New York, and then maybe I'd be going on to Europe. I loved my parents very much, but I was also a committed Zionist. I'd read a book called *The Forgotten Ally* by Pierre van Passen, about the contribution of world Jewry to the defeat of the Nazis – it had opened my eyes and made me very angry. Jews had never been recognised as fighters.

I went to New York, and from there to Baltimore to board a Haganah ship. I went along as a sailor, though I had no experience! First of all we sailed to Marseilles, where the ship was refitted, and then up to Sweden, where we took 650 girl survivors of the camps on board – they had been recuperating in Sweden after their release from the camps. Then, at last, we headed for Palestine via North Africa. Unfortunately the British intercepted us and I was interned for three months on Cyprus, but I got to the homeland in the end. Then, if you can believe it, the Zionists sent me back to Toronto, where my ultimate job was to recruit Jewish boys for the Israel Defence Forces.

Under pressure from the Americans and an increasingly hawkish Ben-Gurion (who had outmanoeuvred the moderate Chaim Weizmann at the 1946 Zionist Congress in Basle), the British Foreign Secretary Ernest Bevin announced on 14 February 1947 that the British Government was going to refer the whole problem of Palestine to the United Nations. Racial tension continued within the country; no one could agree to a way of dividing it in two: the Mandate in its current form was no longer viable: illegal immigration continued despite all efforts to stamp it out; and a solution to the whole mess had to be found. In response the UN set up a Special Committee on Palestine, known as UNSCOP, which was made up of representatives from eleven disinterested member states. The Committee published its report at the end of August, recommending that the Mandate be terminated and Palestine be granted independence as soon as possible; the country should be divided into an Arab and a Jewish state with an independent City of Jerusalem, but retain economic unity. The plan for partition was accepted by the Jewish Agency but, for all the old reasons, rejected by the Arab states. The UN endorsed the plan at the end of November by a majority of two-thirds, which included the USA and the USSR. Britain opposed it.

At the very start of UNSCOP's enquiries, the frustrations of fact-finding became clear. Although the Arab states tried their best to influence UNSCOP their way, the Palestine Arabs washed their hands of the whole procedure, eschewing any likelihood of compromise with the Jews. On the other hand, UNSCOP refused to interview any Jewish underground leaders, though these men were emerging as the most influential in the Jewish community.

All was not lost, however. One member of UNSCOP's staff played a special role in collecting testimony. A black American, Dr Ralph J. Bunche, who had his own feelings of ethnic exclusion, sided fully with the plight of the Jewish people in Palestine and Europe. He was convinced that he had to persuade the Committee to listen to the Zionist militants. Determined to get a clear picture of the problems in Palestine, Bunche arranged a secret meeting with the future Prime Minister, Menachem Begin, then thirty-four years old, a prominent member of the Irgun and regarded by the British as a terrorist.

The meeting took place at a hideout near Tel Aviv. To reduce the risk of being followed, Bunche changed cars several times on his way to the meeting. When he arrived, Begin launched into a passionate speech advocating Jewish statehood in an undivided Palestine. Bunche rejoined with the remark, "I understand you. I am also a member of a persecuted minority." This may not have been the most diplomatic comment for a member of a supposedly disinterested inquiry to have made, but even while UNSCOP were still conducting their investigations in Palestine, the British committed yet another act of intolerance which seemed almost calculated to swing any waverer behind the Jewish cause. In perhaps the best-known single action of the whole troubled period, they turned back a Haganah ship with 4,500 refugees aboard. The ship was the *Exodus 47*. The event formed the basis for Leon Uris' most famous novel, which in turn was made into an extremely ponderous film by Otto Preminger in 1960.

Turning back the *Exodus* gave rise to worldwide protest and must have affected the opinions of at least some of those who would vote at the UN General Assembly in November. Photographs of British troops in full combat gear boarding the ship and using clubs and pistols against the refugees were splashed on the front pages of newspapers all over the globe. As word came out that there were 400 pregnant women on board, determined to give birth to their children in Palestine, few could help being reminded of the German treatment of Jews only a few short years earlier.

The British authorities doubtless thought that they were just turning back another boat; but the damage to their prestige was lasting and the *Exodus* became one of the central symbols of the Jewish struggle for freedom.

Chapter Twenty: *Exodus 47*

Many of those who had miraculously escaped the gas chambers of the concentration camps sought any means possible of getting to the one country which had opened its arms to receive them. Those who had already made their way to France faced the difficult next step of finding a ship to take them to Palestine.

Hanna Zimnowitz had survived the camps and was about to start life with her husband in a DP camp in France when she discovered that they had been lucky enough to secure passages on a ship:

> She was called the *Exodus* and she already had children on board whom the Haganah had picked up throughout Poland – their parents had been left behind, but the hope was that they would join them later. We were told that we'd be in Palestine six days later. Unfortunately, it didn't work out like that.
>
> The *Exodus* had started life as a Mississippi steamer, but she had been stripped clean to make room for as many people as possible and only her beautiful golden staircase remained. Otherwise there were rows and rows of bunks where the cabins had once been. She'd been designed to carry 120 passengers in luxury; now she was carrying 4,500 of us in conditions that were pretty basic!

· Yossi Harel, commander, had intended to pick up refugees in Italy as well as France, but British influence had seen to it that the Italian ports there were closed to him. His ship, originally named the *President Warfield*, was an 1,800-ton four-decker. With full fuel tanks she lay in the French port of Sète as the passengers came aboard. There would be 4,515 of them, men, women and children, all of whom had gone through the hell of the Nazi camps. Six hundred of the children on board were orphans whose parents had died in the gas chambers.

Harel's crew were Jewish Americans, most of them members of the Palmach, and they carried a grave responsibility. Theirs would be the biggest single number of immigrants ever taken by ship to Palestine – the biggest since the Exodus from Egypt. The crew were not experienced seamen, but the Palestine Jews could not afford such a luxury: experience was something one had to make for oneself. Outside the bay, a British destroyer was lurking. The British couldn't touch the *Exodus* in French territorial waters, but the plan was to sail at night in an attempt to give the Royal Navy the slip in any case.

At last they were ready to depart – the pilot they had commissioned hadn't turned up, but they had to go now or they would miss the night tide. Harel decided to do without a pilot. Slowly the ship gathered momentum, but soon afterwards a steel cable snagged one of the propellers and Harel had to reverse engines to clear it: he succeeded, but the manoeuvre had taken thirty precious minutes. Hardly had they got under way again than the ship suddenly shuddered and came to a stop: they had veered too far to the right and had struck a sandbar. Ahead lay the open sea, but they were immobile and the darkness they depended on to make good their escape would soon give way to dawn. Harel ordered the powerful engines full ahead: the *Exodus* strained frighteningly, but at last shook herself free.

As she headed out to sea on an eastward course, the feeling on board was one of exhilaration. The mid-July weather was good, and although they had not been able to duck the attention of the Royal Navy, a strange sense of confidence began to grow in everyone on board. Two babies were born on the first night at sea, and they took this as a good omen. The calm waters soon grew choppy, however, as the wind rose, and many, aboard a ship for the first time, were sick. To make matters worse, the destroyer which was shadowing them had now been joined by two others and by the cruiser *Ajax*, which lost no time in signalling to the *Exodus*: "If you are carrying immigrants, you are acting illegally. We will imprison you as soon as you reach British territorial waters." It seemed that Ernest Bevin, perhaps under pressure from his military advisors, was determined to make an example of this latest attempt by the Zionists to bypass the quota.

On the fourth day another child was born, but its mother died, plunging the passengers into gloom. The poor woman, who had survived a living hell only to die on the threshold of the homeland, was wrapped in the blue and white flag of Israel and buried at sea.

The Royal Navy continued to dog them and by the time she passed the Egyptian coast the *Exodus* had an escort of five destroyers and the *Ajax*. Boarding seemed inevitable, but the refugees prepared themselves to repel any attack.

As the *Exodus* approached Tel Aviv the spirits of those aboard rose again: two Palmach brigades were waiting on shore to aid them, and as the ship had been built for river work, she had a far shallower draught than the warships, which could not follow her close inshore. But the commander of the destroyer *Chequers* took the decision to lie alongside the refugee ship while there was still time, and to board her at sea. At 7.30 p.m. on 17 July, the British warships began to deploy. The *Ajax* was to cut off any route to the shore, while the others would catch the *Exodus* in their searchlights as she was boarded.

The rendezvous with the Palmach forces on shore had been scheduled for 9 a.m. on 18 July; now it looked as if that rendezvous could not be kept. The question was, would the rest of the world care about the plight of the refugees on the *Exodus*? There was nothing to be lost in letting it know. A message was sent in Hebrew, French and English from the ship's radio and broadcast via the Haganah transmitter in Palestine:

"Listen to the immigrant ship *Exodus*, a ship of the Hebrew Haganah, now nearing the shores of Eretz Israël. We are about sixty miles away, and each moment brings us closer to the coast we yearn for. Five British destroyers and one cruiser have us tightly encircled . . ."

The news spread through Palestine and outwards to the rest of the world as the British closed in. By now the entire group of ships was very near the shore. On board the *Exodus*, the women and children were moved to the relative safety of the upper decks. The ship sounded her siren, and at the signal 1,000 young refugees appeared on deck, ready to defend her even though the only weapons they had were sticks or cans of tinned food. It was just before dawn on 18 July when the *Exodus* was flooded with light from the warships and a voice rang out from unseen loudspeakers: "Heave to. You are under arrest!" Hanna Zimnowitz watched:

> As we approached the waters of Palestine, they came so close to us that they started to shout. They said that the women and children would be transferred to their ship, and that they would then tow our ship into harbour.
>
> None of us wanted to move. They became angry and started to yell at us then. Soon afterwards, they threw ropes across and pulled alongside. When the British soldiers began to board, the Haganah told us to try to get their weapons from them and throw them into the sea.
>
> It was growing light by now and the people on the shore could see clearly what was happening. The British ships rammed us and holed us. Water began to pour in. People were panicking but we kept going and we finally made it into the harbour at Haifa. They didn't let us land.

In fact the battle had been even more violent. The British had strafed the *Exodus* with machine-guns, and in the general mêlée three refugees were killed and at least twenty-eight others seriously wounded. The refugees defended themselves fiercely, and even some of the children hurled tin cans at the heads of the soldiers trying to take over their ship. The British responded with tear-gas.

It was inevitable that the British would win, and by the time they had control of the bridge of the *Exodus* the battle was as good as over. As an exercise, however, the British had used far more force than was necessary, and in diplomatic terms the whole episode was a disaster. The battle had taken place in full view of the shore and had been observed by, among others, delegates of UNSCOP. The refugees, who enjoyed the sympathy of virtually the whole non-Arab world, were transferred to three British ships and held prisoner on them. Some of the *Exodus'* crew managed to escape and make contact with the Haganah on shore. The *Exodus* herself, battered but still proud, lay in the port at Haifa as a reproach to Britain and an inspiration to Palestine Jews.

Ernest Bevin, however, seemed bent on compounding the mess. He decided that these refugees would not be sent to Cyprus, but returned to France – the three ships with the would-be immigrants on board were ordered to sail to Port-de-Bouc. The immigrants were not even allowed to retrieve their belongings. Hanna Zimnowitz remembers:

> We had nothing – just what we were wearing. They'd erected chicken-wire fences around us to keep us prisoner. In protest, we started a hunger strike and threw their food overboard. Only the children ate.
>
> There were so many people on our boat. No place to sleep – there was fighting at night for a small space to lie down. No water, either. It was horrible. And we had 600 children with us.

They arrived back in French waters on 29 July. The French offered the refugees asylum if they wished to land, but the Jews wanted to go to Palestine and they refused to disembark. Bevin tried to persuade the French authorities to force the refugees to go ashore, but this the French angrily refused to do. Meanwhile, anti-British feeling was rising by the day. The battle off Haifa was being shown on newsreels all over Europe and the USA. There had been a huge demonstration in New York. The British embassies in Washington and Paris were sending urgent communiqués to the Foreign Office to limit the damage that had already been done. But Bevin was inflexible. The ships carrying the refugees were ordered to sail to Germany, of all places, and there the passengers were indeed forcibly disembarked and taken to a DP camp at Poppendorf, near Lübeck. Not only were these survivors of the concentration camps in Germany, but they had been put into a DP camp which was, as Hanna Zimnowitz recalled, a former concentration camp itself!

Of course the whole horrible sequence of events had been closely followed by the world press. One report for 8 September 1947 ran: "British troops today landed 1,400 screaming, kicking and weeping Jewish refugees from the transport *Ocean Vigour*, using physical force to compel recalcitrant passengers to set foot on German soil. Truncheons were employed unsparingly."

If the story of the *Exodus* can be said to have a happy ending, it lies in the endurance and determination of her passengers, whose plight won them sympathy worldwide. In the end, they all found their way to Palestine, though some did not get there until after the State of Israel had been founded. By their actions during the two-month saga of the *Exodus*, the British might have been working hand-in-glove with the Zionist propaganda machine.

Hanna Zimnowitz escaped from Poppendorf with her husband and, with the help of the Haganah, made her way back to the homeland again – this time successfully. The voyage on the *Exodus*, by the way, had been her honeymoon – and she had never before been on a ship, or even seen the sea!

Chapter Twenty-One: Terror

UNSCOP's findings closely followed those of the Peel Commission a few years earlier; it was as if nothing had changed – except, perhaps, that there was now an even greater sense of urgency in the air. The Second World War had been won at a price for Britain: it had lost 30 per cent of its reserves, its factories were either bombed or outmoded, and above all what had remained of its power as a world state was ebbing fast. The power centres of the world were now in Washington and Moscow.

In Jewish Palestine, young men driven by the sense of urgency were in positions to do something about getting things done – and the ends justified the means. Two future Prime Ministers, Yitzhak Shamir, now back from exile, and Menachem Begin, headed the Stern Gang and the Irgun respectively. Both men had tragic pasts: Begin had been chased out of his native Poland by the Nazis, thrown in prison by the Russians, hunted down by the British and almost murdered by the Jews. Shamir had lost every one of his relatives in the Holocaust. Both were viewed variously as fanatic, terrorist, zealot and killer; or as patriot and revolutionary. Their shared aim was to drive the British from their homeland. From 1944 to 1948 the Irgun and the Stern Gang would blow up British installations, steal British arms, break prisoners out of jail, and flog and even hang British soldiers. By the end of 1946, Jewish assassins had claimed 373 victims. They earned the opprobrium of the press and were in constant danger from informers. Not every Jew approved of their methods.

Begin's defence of his actions was always the same: the fight was against the British and the Arabs, and the conditions were those of a war. It was a strict rule of the Irgun that, whatever happened, no member should ever take arms against a fellow Jew. One of their most ambitious actions was the one they took against Acre jail.

This British prison was well known to both Begin and Shamir. Shamir had spent time there as a prisoner in 1942:

> It was not a very pleasant experience. Acre jail was in an old fort and it was very overcrowded. The moment I arrived they shaved my head and took away my shoelaces. Then they told me to strip and handed me the "uniform" of another prisoner whom they'd just released.

The prison had the reputation of being the best guarded in Palestine. At the time of the planned attack it held about one hundred members of the Irgun, the Stern Gang and the Haganah. On its gallows convicted Jewish terrorists were hanged. Acre itself was an Arab city surrounded by three British military camps. Because it seemed so impregnable, security may have been slack.

The attack was set for 4 May 1947. Units of the Irgun approached the prison in daylight, dressed in British army uniforms and driving captured British military vehicles. They arrived at the prison unchallenged; the guards were watching a game of handball that had been prearranged as a diversion.

Once the Irgun were in the courtyard of the jail, they rapidly laid an explosive charge around a large barred window. The noise of the explosion was the first hint the guards had that an attack was taking place, but before they could react, prisoners began to stream out of the ragged oblong hole that had been made in the wall. However, the Irgun had reckoned without the unforeseen presence of an extra British unit in the vicinity. These soldiers, returning from a swim, reacted quickly and were soon engaged in fierce combat with the Jewish freedom fighters. Nine members of the Irgun team were killed, including their young commander, Dov Cohen, and three more were taken prisoner. Forty-one prisoners escaped, though not without fatalities.

The break had been planned in co-ordination with those inside the jail. One of the prisoners was Menachem Malatzky, the area Irgun commander for Haifa, who'd been arrested earlier in the year:

The break was going to take place during the exercise period, when all the cell doors would be open. I was one of the ones doing their share on the inside. We had to dig a tunnel and prepare the explosives that had been smuggled in to us. The Irgun on the outside arrived dressed as British soldiers, with a jeep and three trucks for us to escape in.

Smuggling things in had to be planned carefully. Our people on the outside were going to blow a hole in the outer wall, but we had to blow out two iron doors which barred our way to the wall. It was the time of Passover, and on the last day of Passover the prisoners had the privilege of receiving visitors who could bring gifts of cake and chocolate and so on. The British allowed some of us European Jews greater freedom and special privileges in the prison: we could wear civilian clothes and we were allowed to see our visitors without bars between us.

On the last day of Passover one of our Irgun girls on the outside came to visit me from Haifa and brought with her a big carton of Players cigarettes. The tobacco had been taken out of the cigarettes and replaced with detonators. When I went back to my cell I was searched by a guard. I showed him the carton and said, "Look! How about that? A beautiful carton of cigarettes!" He was happy for me.

The plan now was for about forty of us to escape. There were well over eighty of us in the prison, but those on the outside couldn't handle a break that big. Three of us had to select who should go and who should stay. It was a heartbreaking job but it had to be done and of course we had to choose the men who'd be most useful in our continuing fight. Most of the men selected were senior officers. Next, we divided ourselves into three groups. The first was thirteen in number. Their job was to blow a way out to the outer wall. The second group, of twenty, had to pour kerosene on the floor and be ready to light it to cause a fire which would prevent police reinforcements closing off our escape. The third unit consisted of eight people armed with grenades: this was our rearguard.

At 4.20 p.m. on 4 May we heard the explosion outside. Everyone in the first unit, which I commanded, knew what to do. We had to blow out a barred entrance first, and then the iron doors. Then we saw the hole in the outer wall and made for it. Arab prisoners were taking advantage of it and rushing out too. They took off in one direction, we in another.

We were out within three or four minutes, but unfortunately we ran straight into a British unit which shouldn't have been there at all, and they began shooting at us. In the confusion we made for a car, but they sprayed the car with bullets.

Of the original thirteen, five were killed and seven were wounded. I was shot in the leg and couldn't run, and although I made it to a ditch they recaptured me there. They took us back to jail, but none of us got medical treatment for six hours. We were made to lie on the floor and one of my friends died there of his wounds. I said, "You have to treat us like prisoners of war." For that I got a kick in the face.

The three captured members of the Irgun assault team were hanged by the British on 29 July – the same day that the *Exodus* arrived back in France. But if the British thought that this would serve as a deterrent, they were wrong. The Irgun hit back with a vengeance. They had kidnapped two British army sergeants, Clifford Martin and Mervin Paice, as they were leaving a café in Natanya. Two days after the execution of the Irgun fighters, the bodies of Martin and Paice were found hanging in a eucalyptus copse. Irgun execution orders were pinned on them. Worse was to come. When British soldiers arrived to cut the bodies down, one of the corpses blew to bits and an officer was wounded: the Irgun had mined the area.

This action caused another furore around the world, whose press was already whipped up by the *Exodus* affair. In Britain, the left-wing *Manchester Guardian* carried an article which ran: "The time has come for (the) government to leave Palestine." The gallows were not used again. Very soon, the British would cease to hold a Mandate to govern in Palestine. UNSCOP proposed a gradual withdrawal of all British forces, to be completed by 1 August 1948 at the latest.

The threat of execution had in any case been no deterrent to the young men and women who volunteered for the Irgun and the Stern Gang. If tried and sentenced, moreover, they refused to recognise the court and thus went to their deaths without speaking in their defence or appealing against sentence. On their way to the gallows, many sang the *Hatikvah*. "Avenge our blood!" cried the three Irgun hanged after the Acre jailbreak. Meir Feinstein and Moshe Barazani blew themselves up with a grenade the night before they were due to be executed, preferring suicide to death at the hands of the hated British. Morale among those who served the British regime faltered.

Chapter Twenty-Two: False Dawn

When the General Assembly of the United Nations broadly approved the recommendations of UNSCOP's report· by a two-thirds majority on 29 November 1947, there was great rejoicing among the Jews of Palestine. The UN had recognised that a Jewish state should exist, and the uneasy rule of Britain in Palestine was effectively at an end. Of course the rejoicing was clouded by the knowledge that the Arab states were against the recommendations, but that was hardly surprising and the Jews knew that they could stand their ground if they had to. There was still much to do and probably more blood would be spilt before peace and security could finally be achieved; but there was a general feeling that a corner had been turned.

For the days immediately following the UN endorsement, there was dancing in the streets. The *Palestine Post* reported that "the Zionist flag could be seen draped from buildings, strung from lampposts, and fluttering from cars and trucks. Lorry-loads of singing youngsters careered through the streets . . ."

Channa Levi from Pennsylvania was in Palestine when the news broke:

Our youth group was about to disband, since our visit was coming to an end and various members were going their separate ways. We had a farewell party, and while the party was going on, one of the men from the room next door came rushing in and said, "The decision for partition has been made!" and we all drank to it. We thought about waking the children to let them know, but we decided to let them sleep.

I hardly slept myself – none of us did – and I remember having a sore head when I woke up. It was still dark, and I could hear the ringing of a triangle. I looked out of my window and saw all these little children running out and dancing in celebration. Fifteen years later, I met a man who was at the same place then and told him the story. He said, "I rang the triangle."

As the sun came up on 30 November, the party continued, with happy revellers cheerfully invading the homes of anyone who'd let them in. In the cities, the cafés were overflowing, and not a few British soldiers and policemen joined in, in a spirit of what must have been relief. But as the details of the plan filtered through, many people paused for thought. Palestine had been partitioned in a complicated manner that didn't seem likely to satisfy anyone for long. The hope that Arabs and Jews could live peacefully side by side was still a desperate one, and although such leaders as Ben-Gurion had gone along with the UN proposals, they had done so for the sake of seeing the immigration restrictions lifted: at least now those refugee Jews still trapped in Europe could come to the homeland without hindrance.

As Ben-Gurion watched the scenes of rejoicing from his Tel Aviv office window, he was all too aware that the Arab nations would not simply sit back and allow a Jewish state to come into being; and indeed a response from the Arabs was not long in coming. The Arab Higher Committee was furious at the UN decision and immediately set about posting notices in Jerusalem calling for a three-day strike from 1 December, together with a boycott of Jewish shops and businesses. Arab demonstrators protested outside the consulates of those countries which had voted in favour of the proposals, throwing stones and yelling anti-Jewish slogans. Two hundred Arab youths marched on the centre of Jerusalem. Chanting "Death to the Jews", they made their way to the Jaffa Gate and broke into a number of Jewish shops, looting some and setting others ablaze.

The British authorities did nothing to stop the demonstrators, and later reports indicated that some British soldiers had themselves been involved in the looting. At the end of the day, the only arrests that were made were of sixteen members of the Haganah who were found with weapons, though some distance from the scene of the disturbances. The Jewish leadership declared, however, that any further acts of aggression of this nature against the Jews would be met with force.

The feelings of rage at British inaction on this occasion soon dissolved. Nearby, in Talpiyot, five Jewish buses had been attacked by an Arab mob. Loss of life had been averted by the prompt intervention of a British inspector of police and his men.

There was no time to harbour grudges against the British now in any case: they would soon be leaving. Some felt that their presence, although never welcome, had at least held the Arabs in check. Once the British had gone, the threat of all-out war would almost certainly be realised.

Chapter Twenty-Three:
Rumours of War

Early in December Britain announced that it would continue to rule Palestine until 15 May 1948, when its Mandate would end. In the meantime, it would do nothing to implement the partition plans laid down by the UN – presumably because of the cost and chaos such implementation would bring in its wake. There was also some cynical *Realpolitik* going on here: while hindering Jewish attempts at amassing weapons, the British actually sold them to the neighbouring Arab states, and Britain's long association with Arab nations was personified in John Bagot Glubb – "Glubb Pasha" – who had spent a lifetime of service in Iraq and Transjordan. In the latter country he had organised the Arab Legion in 1930, and had commanded it since 1939.

From the time of the British declaration until the foundation of the State of Israel, an unofficial war was waged between Jews and Arabs, in which the British did not intervene officially. It was formalised immediately after the State was proclaimed.

Most of the Palestine Jews felt that however displeased the Arabs might be, they at least had countries of their own. The Jews still had nothing but a promise and, to make their situation worse, they were surrounded by the armies of Egypt, Lebanon, Syria, Iraq, Saudi Arabia and Jordan, all of which were ready for war and determined to reverse the UN decision. A summit in Cairo resolved that the Arab states would "do everything possible to bring about the collapse of the United Nations partition plan".

Acts of Arab terrorism within Palestine started immediately. A bus carrying Jews to Jerusalem was blown up and another ambushed. Armed bands began crossing the borders from neighbouring Arab states. Military forays were made against Jewish settlements close to frontiers. By the end of the first week, over 100 Jews had been killed and many more injured. There were rumours of military training being stepped up in Damascus. The Jews braced themselves. They would certainly not give up without a fight, and their land was worth fighting for. Channa Levi remembers her own feelings, and she hadn't been forced to emigrate from a ruined Europe, but had come voluntarily from the USA:

> The walk up Mount Carmel and the beautiful spring flowers simply captivated me. I suddenly felt that I could live so well in these surroundings. Pennsylvania suddenly seemed very dull.

Although she was to live through an exciting time in Palestine, she wasn't prepared for the conditions that existed in the hinterland, and especially not in the place where she was to make her temporary home:

> Ra'ananna was a one-horse town in those days, with one long street and a post-office. The town had been founded by an American and the first night we were there the mayor came and spoke to us in Hebrew, of which I understood maybe four words: International Ladies' Garment Union! It seems that they were the people who'd backed the group who'd settled the place.
>
> There was a curfew at that time, but we had a wonderful five months based there, and we were very special, since we were the first American group to come there. We lived in wooden huts, though, and the first horror was that there were no screens on the windows. When we asked why, the locals asked us what screens were! We said, "We can't possibly live here without screens", so they decided to find us some and eventually we got them. The other shock was the outside lavatory, which had a flush all right, but you had to put the used

paper in a bucket next to the pan. Luckily there was a kind of janitor who took the paper away and burnt it. We were horrified at first, it was all so primitive – but of course you can get used to anything.

We were three to a room. Most of the time I had diarrhoea and ended up eating rice and horrible things like that. There was very little meat. But we learnt to adapt. We learnt that Noël Coward was dead right when he wrote that only "mad dogs and Englishmen go out in the midday sun", and we also learnt that drinking hot tea cools you down.

We had Hebrew classes, for which we were divided into three levels. I was in the middle level, which only goes to show how little some of the others knew. We also had a dancing teacher. But, you know, we were really special to the people there. We stood out. You'd see people looking at our clothes and whispering, "Americanas!"

Despite the drawbacks, we did have a marvellous time. We had our own bus with our own driver and we toured the country in it. But the minute the sun went down you had to obey the rules of the curfew and get off the streets and into your house.

I must say I understood the Arabs' point of view, but especially when it came to British soldiers! We'd decided that as Jewish girls we'd make life as rotten as possible for the tommies. But they'd always be at us, stopping the bus and checking our papers. Our leader had a letter from the Jewish Agency which covered all of us and said why we were there and what we were doing, but that was never enough for the British. We had to have our passports with us all the time. The soldiers would always be asking, "What are you doing here?" And we'd say, "We're here because we want to be – unlike you!"

They hated it in Palestine. They were all young boys, red from the sun and lonely. They knew they were hated. Since most of the women wouldn't date them they had a lousy time, they missed their families and they hated what they were doing. Whenever we reached a guard post we'd start singing "Be it never so humble, there's no place like home", just to make them feel worse!

We actually had the greatest time imaginable. We visited sixty kibbutzim, and we even got down to the Negev, to see them laying the water lines. One of the arrangements that had been made for us was that we would spend several weeks with the Hadassah nurses studying on Mount Scopus. We watched them at work and studied first aid with them. Most of them were young women of about our age, and we thought they were just the greatest! But it was the coldest place I think I have ever been in. They had practically no heating. But that was the way people lived then. It was just marvellous!

After the first six months of our stay were over, we were asked what we wanted to do with the other half of our year. Most of us wanted to work on a kibbutz. I decided that I would go to one which had the leading dance troupe in the country and study dancing with them. But meanwhile I had fallen in love and so I went to the kibbutz my boyfriend belonged to.

We worked with the children at Shefayyim. That was a lovely period. These were kids who had come from Europe, but also at that time we were beginning to bring in children from North Africa who had also come in with the Youth Aliyah. It was a marvellous place to be.

Whilst preparing for war, the Jewish leadership also had to map out the constitution of their new democratic state. If it ever came into being, it would have to have an infrastructure and a legal system ready for it. Ben-Gurion approached a brilliant young lawyer called Hirim Cohen and charged him with leading a special commission to prepare a legislative system:

Why me? I wondered. There were plenty of lawyers much more experienced than I was. But I did have the reputation of being an expert in Jewish law, and that was what they wanted to base the new legislature on. So I was called in and put in charge of preparing the basic laws of the new state. I had a group of five or six colleagues working with me.

We had fewer than six months to do the job, since Ben-Gurion had made it plain that independence would be proclaimed as soon as the British departed. I cannot say that we worked day and night because at night we had to do our military service – we were already living in a state of siege, and every citizen had to do guard duty at night. And during the day I was drafting laws.

One day I had a call from my military commander. He wanted me to include in the legislation a law to punish soldiers found looting Arab property. Since I could write anything I wanted and it would become law immediately, without having to pass through any parliament, I drafted one and incorporated it into the rest of the new system. That same night, when I had to go on guard duty, I found that it was very cold. My father-in-law was concerned for me and threw his heavy fur coat around my shoulders. I wore it all night, but the next morning I was arrested. The officer of the guard wouldn't believe that I'd been lent the coat and so he was charging me with looting!

Haim Cohen spent only one night in jail, but the atmosphere outside might have made him wish he could have stayed longer. Tension was rising as the Arabs resolved to make a last attempt to rid Palestine of the Jews before their position there became formalised. At the time, Liesl Katz was working for the British Overseas Airways Corporation at Lydda Airport:

I shared an office with an Egyptian Jew and an Arab who had married a Jew. One Friday, we had to travel to Rishon, and we were offered a lift, in one of a new type of car that the company had acquired, as far as Tel Aviv. These cars were very long and they were nicknamed "snakes". There were no weapons on board but the cars were very fast and the driver assured us that he could get us out of any trouble. We got to Tel Aviv safely and said goodbye; but that evening we heard on the radio that the same car had been ambushed and everyone in it had been killed.

Fighting throughout the region was becoming less sporadic and more regular. It was time for Channa Levi to take up arms:

For the next few months a group of about thirty of us learned how to use a gun. By the end of that time I could handle a Czech rifle, though I was pretty sure I'd never be able to kill anyone with it. Still, we took turns at guard duty and every time I was scared. We slept in our clothes because we never knew when an attack might come. I remember that we were in a pretty basic encampment near a railway track, which we were supposed to be guarding. Every evening when I kissed my boyfriend goodnight I said, "Do you think we'll wake up dead?" "Be positive," he replied.

Later on we became engaged and had a party to celebrate, but I sprained my ankle dancing. The following day I remember that there was going to be a concert with gramophone records, which believe it or not was a real event in those days, so I hobbled through the mud – it had been raining real heavy – to the place where the concert was.

During the concert they started shooting at us – I noticed the girl next to me had been shot in the leg before she realised it herself, and I pulled her down to take cover under a table. It was chaos. We weren't far from an Arab village and it didn't seem to be very clear which side had started shooting first. There was a British base not far away and we knew that pretty soon they would come over and start asking questions, so we decided to pretend that none of us could speak English, because we certainly didn't want to co-operate with them. Their translator didn't know we could understand every word he was saying. Luckily we'd got someone from the Haganah to take care of the wounded girl before the British arrived, and we'd shoved a table against the wall where the bullet-hole was.

Even so the whole story got into the papers and the people in charge of our course told us Americans that it was too dangerous for us to stay in the country any longer. Anyway, they said, you'll be of more value to us back in the States, letting them know what's been happening here. So we left by armoured bus for Tel Aviv.

By then, though, there were no ships for the USA, and there were no planes either, because there'd been shooting at the airport. We didn't know how we'd get out of the country, and by that time too communications between Tel Aviv and Jerusalem had been cut. Our group leader had to travel to Jerusalem by armoured bus to get some papers he needed from the American Embassy there. That was the day the Arabs blew up the Jewish Agency offices, but he was all right and managed to get back to Tel Aviv in one piece with his documents.

We had enough money to leave by ship but not by air. However, we'd met a nice woman who'd worked for the Hadassah and she suggested that we call at her office in the bank where she worked, and she'd see what she could do for us. When we made our way there we saw that the whole street where the bank was had been cordoned off. There was a group of what looked like British soldiers and they told us that they were going to make a withdrawal at the bank. I should have guessed at once from their accents that they weren't British soldiers at all, but Irgun, and that they were going to rob the bank.

In the end Channa and her companions were able to get a flight back to the States; but it was years before she realised that she was the only one of their number who was *not* travelling there to buy guns.

As 1947 drew to a close, most Jews living in Palestine looked back on a hard year. Many still had friends and relatives in internment on Cyprus or trapped in the DP camps of Europe, and these were never far from the thoughts of those who had successfully made the Aliyah. On the other hand, hearts lifted at the thought of how close the people were to the realisation of an internationally recognised Jewish state.

Everyone looked towards the diminutive, energetic figure of David Ben-Gurion, with his mane of white hair. He had never swayed from his purpose, and still he worked tirelessly both to lay the foundation stones of that state and to build an army to defend it. His vision inspired his people.

Chapter Twenty-Four: Inferno

There is still a strong division of opinion about whether or not it was necessary for the Irgun and the Stern Gang to conduct a terror campaign in order to drive the British out of Palestine. Terrorism has been defined as the weapon of the weak, and those who support the conduct of Begin, Shamir and their followers will say that it was born of frustration and rage, and that any means to ensure the safety of Jewry by establishing a state for it were justified.

Kalman Perk survived the concentration camps and made his way to Palestine after the war, where he was detained by the British for a short time:

I was one of the first youths to come out of Nazi Germany and I suppose at that age kids don't think too clearly. I thought that Palestine wasn't all that it could be and I rebelled against the fact that the British ruled it.

That led me to make contact with the Stern Group. Its real name was LEHI – *Lohame Herut Israël* – Fighters for the Freedom of Israel. They accepted me as a member and in the course of time I was promoted. It was a properly run military unit – we weren't just crazy bombers. I don't know if I can say that I contributed very much, but I felt good about what I was doing. I believed strongly that it had to be done. Nowadays the word "idealistic" is out of fashion.

Today, people remember the Stern people as terrorists; but when I was with them, we were idealists.

My classmates knew I was part of Stern, but that wasn't a problem. I did, however, have some difficulty with the school staff. The headmaster called me in and told me that if I was actively involved in the Irgun, I would have to leave the school. I told him truthfully that I wasn't, and he accepted my word and let me stay on. He was a patriot, too.

Begin and Shamir argued that neither Irgun nor Stern injured fellow Jews, and that what acts of violence they did commit – such as the hanging of the two British sergeants – were acts of retaliation, which were also intended to show the British and the Arabs that the Jews had teeth. Ben-Gurion did not agree. He was convinced that such acts of terror did little to encourage support for the Jews overseas. However, Arab attacks on Jewish settlements, and the threat of a conventional war with neighbouring Arab states following Britain's departure, equally convinced him of the need to build up a proper defence force to protect them, and he realised that such a defence force could best be developed out of the old Haganah. The Haganah began a recruitment campaign. Among those approached for training were Bianca Romano-Segre and her husband:

I felt it was quite natural. We attended all the drills and learnt how to use a rifle in the orange groves. I was very proud to be a member of Haganah. Most of our friends during training were other Italians and some Romanians with whom we could communicate because a lot of them spoke French. Later on, of course, as our command of Hebrew got better, we could mix with more and more people, but in the early days not speaking German cut you off from a lot of your fellows.

The opening months of 1948 saw a continuation of the acts of violence which had run through the previous year. The *Palestine Post*, the only English-language newspaper in the country, was preparing for the next day's edition when a bomb exploded at its offices, killing four members of staff and injuring many others. The survivors still managed to bring out a reduced edition, with the headline: "The *Palestine Post* Appears Today

In Another Format; But It Appears!" The bomb had been made by two British deserters, Captain Eddie Brown and Corporal Peter Marsden, who had joined forces with a group of Arab "irregulars". They later stated that they had intended to blow up the Zion Hall Cinema, but by the time they arrived the film was over and the audience had left, so they decided to blow up the *Post*'s offices because they knew that there would be people there.

Such acts of violence could not be ignored by the militant Jewish groups, however much Ben-Gurion might continue to plead for restraint and moderation; both the Irgun and the Stern Gang grew in size, being joined among others by former members of the Haganah. At the same time, the UN, which had no peace-keeping force to deploy in Palestine to enforce policy and which did not enjoy the support of the British – who maintained their stated policy of non-intervention (though tacitly siding with the Arabs) – now began to have second thoughts about partition. The threat of all-out war was apparent to everyone, and the Arab states were growing more hawkish by the day.

The UN began to put out feelers: what did member states feel about the possibility of putting Palestine once again under the mandatory rule of an existing nation? Ben-Gurion was quick to react; he declared that his people were strongly opposed to "any proposal that would prevent or postpone the establishment of a Jewish state".

Time was running out. If the Jews were ever to have a country they could call their own, they would have to act now by speeding up their organisation of a Jewish administration. In his office in Tel Aviv, Ben-Gurion began to receive various Zionist leaders with a view to appointing a provisional government to step in when the British left.

There would be two governing bodies, one composed of thirty-seven people and the other of thirteen. These would be known respectively as the National Council and the National Executive, and they would hold joint responsibility for governing the country until such time as democratic elections could be held. During this interim period, Ben-Gurion himself would act as Prime Minister and Defence Minister.

Ben-Gurion summoned Haim Cohen to give a progress report on the new legislation:

> I went to his house, and when I was admitted to the room where he was, I saw that he was lying on the sofa with no clothes on. He wasn't in the least bit embarrassed. He told me to sit down and describe all the new laws we had prepared. I asked him if I should get him a blanket or something, but he shook his head. I stayed with him for three hours – me and a naked Ben-Gurion, discussing the new set of laws that we were making and planning!

Now, every day brought fresh outbreaks of violence, and it was clear that nothing could be gained by remaining on the defensive. The Palestine Jews realised that they would have to step up their armaments programme. Secret munitions and weapons factories were set up, and Palmach units made sorties into Arab villages and camps to seize weapons and ammunition from them. They would also attack and destroy any Arab terrorist or quasi-military centre they found. These night assaults demoralised many Arab inhabitants, some of whom moved away. Weapons were also solicited from abroad, and an especially good source of supply was the United States, with its large and powerful Jewish population. Because of Anglo-American embargoes, however, these weapons had to be smuggled into Palestine.

In the midst of all this, new immigrants were still arriving. Marlin and Betty Levin had spent some time working in Europe and the Far East before leaving their native New York for Palestine:

> Our packing cases were disembarked with us at Haifa, but before I could clear them I had to go through a kind of mini-interrogation with a British officer. The removal company that had packed our things had used old World War Two arms crates which had things like "fuses", "bombs" and "mortars" written on their sides. As practically everyone in the country was throwing grenades at each other at the time it wasn't exactly clever of us to arrive with our stuff in munitions chests – but we hadn't been around when they'd been packed. The British officer opened the crates and when he saw

that they contained pots and pans and so forth he calmed down a bit and said to me, "Funny kind of joke."

We stayed in Haifa for a day and then made our way with some friends from the ship on a rickety bus to Jerusalem. The countryside looked very beautiful, but when we passed a group of Arabs, they threw stones at the bus. It didn't matter. We'd fallen in love with the country as soon as we'd seen the white buildings of Haifa from the ship.

The bus chugged into Jerusalem and stopped on Jaffa Road. On the pavement was a little Arab boy who looked at me and waved a newspaper. "Idiot, idiot!" he yelled. I couldn't help feeling that these were exactly the sentiments of our New York friends when we told them that we were going to live in Palestine. Of course later on I found that he wasn't calling me names at all. What he was yelling was "*Yediot*" – the name of the paper he was trying to sell!

We got off the bus with our friends and checked in at a pension. It was Saturday night and I wanted to take a look at downtown Jerusalem, so we started walking down Jaffa Road. As we were walking along my wife noticed someone coming towards us whom she thought we knew, and it just so happened that the guy was an acquaintance of mine from New York. We chatted for a bit and then he asked me what my job was. I told him I was a journalist. He said, "You are? Come with me!"

He grabbed me by the arm and pulled me into a building which housed the offices of the *Palestine Post*. He took me straight in to see the editor. The editor looked at me with a scowl on his face and said, "Who are you?" I told him, and said that my friend had just hauled me in there. "So what do you know about journalism?" he asked. I said that I'd worked on *Women's Wear Journal* and that I had a degree in journalism. He said, "Get in the newsroom and start editing!" "Hang on a minute," I said. "We've just arrived in the country and I'd like to see some of it." "How long do you want?" he said. "Three weeks." "You've got it. But then I want you back here!"

So Betty and I toured the country with a knapsack and a typewriter. In those days taking a trip around Palestine wasn't easy. The Jewish Agency worked an itinerary out for us. On such and such a night we had to stay at such and such a kibbutz, and so on. Most of the time the people had no idea who we were, but they took us in anyway.

Many of them were virtually new arrivals themselves. In some places we slept on the floor; in others, in tents.

When we got back to Jerusalem we rented an apartment from a Christian Arab doctor. Betty got a job as a teacher – at that time any professional American had no trouble finding work – but later on, when the war started, she worked for the Haganah's radio monitoring section. And I, too, joined the Haganah.

One day our landlord, who was a very, very fine gentleman, said to me, "I notice that you have a two-way radio." It was true. I'd actually been looking for an ordinary radio but I'd found this two-way job in an army surplus store and picked it up as a curiosity. "I think the Haganah could find a use for that," he said. It turned out that he had a friend who was an officer in the Haganah. That was quite something. The following day, the officer came round and I gave him the radio. He wanted to give me a receipt and told me the thing would be returned to me, but I told him to keep it.

I was at the *Palestine Post* when the offices were blown up. It was February 1948. I was editing copy and doing some rewriting on a story about one of the latest bombings or shootings when there was a kind of whoosh. Half the street went up in smoke. Luckily we'd heard rumours that something like this might happen, so I'd left my usual desk near the window to sit at the desk of a sub-editor who wasn't on duty that night – his desk was in a corner, protected by two walls. If I'd been in my regular seat I would have been killed, because a huge piece of iron came flying through the window and landed slap on my desk: it would have cut my head off. Our apartment was two or three kilometres away, but Betty told me later that she'd heard the boom. It'd even rattled the windows at home. Right at the centre of the explosion there'd been almost no noise at all.

I helped some of my colleagues out of the building and then went home. I was pretty shaken. It was a cold winter's night but I walked home in my shirt sleeves. I banged on the door for Betty to open up. She'd been in bed and wasn't too pleased. "Don't you have a key?" she said. It was in my jacket back at the office. "Where's your coat?" she said. I said, "Haven't you heard? They just blew up the *Palestine Post*." She almost fainted then.

We shared the apartment with another couple, and the husband was in the Haganah. He'd been on guard duty when he heard about the bomb. As soon as he could, he rushed home and when he saw me, he gave me a big bear hug. "Thank God you're all right." I was shaking like a leaf by then, so he went out for a doctor, who took out a syringe and some tranquillising drug or other, and then started to read the instructions about how to use it. I turned to the Haganah guy and said, "Jack, what kind of doctor is this?" Jack said, "He's the only one I could find." The doctor grinned. It turned out that he was Palestine's leading gynaecologist. I don't know what he gave me, but that night I slept like a baby.

Next morning I went back to the office and I saw that the building was in ruins. Still I was able to get up to the office and when I went over to my desk I could see that the force of the blast had ripped its drawers open. There was broken glass inside. Our presses downstairs were wrecked, so we used the presses of another paper and managed to get an edition out – though only a two-pager! Our editor had survived – but I think it was him the Arabs had really wanted to get.

Things didn't get better quickly. I remember that when the Arab Legion under Glubb Pasha was trying to wrest Jerusalem away from us during the war, we couldn't get back to our apartment because of the shelling. It was a really hairy situation. The editor got us to stay at his place, and he and I would walk to work together every afternoon and home every night. There was no transport, no electricity, no fuel, no water. That editor was a brave man. One day as we were walking along the Arabs started shelling us very heavily and I wanted to get into a bomb shelter. He refused to come with me. He pointed to a shoe-shine man sitting under a cinema awning and he said, "If that man can sit and shine shoes during a shelling, then I'm going to have my shoes shined." I let him get on with it. By the time I came out of the shelter, he'd already gone back to work.

When Ben Dunkelman went over from Canada, he arrived at Marseilles to be told that as he was going in illegally, he would have to have a new identity:

It was a strange experience; I'd never done anything illegal or undercover before, and here I was, giving up my own name and nationality and taking over someone else's! When I got my new passport, I found that I was now an Englishman from Twickenham called Fox, 5 feet 8 inches tall, 160 lb in weight, with brown eyes and dark hair. My difficulty in assuming this identity will be understood if I mention that I am 6 feet 2 inches, weighed close on 240 lb then, and have blue eyes and fair hair. Apart from that, we might have been twins!

Getting to Palestine to fight was the second problem Gordon Quitt faced. The first was getting out of Canada, because the US customs officers regarded him with suspicion. He and his group finally made it to New York:

We went directly to the hotel where we were expected and given rooms after we had handed in our passports at reception. Then we were told to go to a place on Cypress Avenue where we would be contacted. There we met another group of people including a Jewish Palestinian who was going to be our leader. His name was Moishe Shifron.

We had to wait a while, but in the end we got a ship which was bound for Marseilles and Genoa – the SS *Sobieski*, a Polish liner. There were forty-five of us on board in various cabins. We were told not to draw attention to ourselves, so we kept our heads down, but we still had a great time on the crossing. We disembarked at Marseilles and were taken from there to a place up in the Alps called Ste Thérèse. There we were billeted in an old fortified mansion with maybe twenty rooms in all, and began our military training. We had no weapons, but we did a lot of tough work-outs. One guy, from Denmark or Holland I think, actually went mad. I don't know what happened or what they did with him after they'd taken him away, but boy, I've never met anyone quite so strong. I weighed all of 136 lb and he could just lift me up with one arm, no problem.

After the training course we returned to Marseilles and one night embarked on an immigrant ship. There were boys on board I recognised from Toronto – real kids, with absolutely no idea of how to handle a gun or anything. There were some girls, too, mostly from Britain.

We set off and made good time, but when we reached the Straits of Messina the engines broke down. We had to stay below while they were being fixed, and the crew kept scanning the horizon with binoculars, on the lookout for British ships. We finally got going again, but the whole voyage took maybe fifteen days.

When we arrived in Palestine it was a shock to discover that there was no army *per se*. Nobody seemed to know anything, or what to do with us.

Quitt finally got a job as a driver for the Air Force, delivering bombs and ammunition. Meanwhile, the violence continued, and reached its peak in two acts of appalling atrocity.

The village of Deir Yassin no longer exists. In early April 1948 it was an Arab settlement overlooking the strategically important Jerusalem–Tel Aviv road and guarding the approach to Jerusalem. It was well placed, therefore, to serve as a centre for Arab terrorist activities and it was also used as a base for covert operations by the Arab Legion and the Iraqi Army. On 9 April, in the belief that an Arab force was sheltering in the village, the Irgun launched an all-out assault and in the process killed 250 Arab civilians, including many women and children.

The facts of the Deir Yassin massacre remain a matter of hot debate, and the event is still political dynamite. A Jewish survey of 1987 argues that the number killed was only about 110; Menachem Begin, who probably ordered the attack, states in his memoirs that warning was given to civilians to leave prior to the attack and that many, in fact, did so. Arab commentators have suggested that the civilians were wilfully killed, and that view is shared by many Jews who did not support the extremist organisations; Begin always maintained that they were shot unintentionally as the Irgun flushed out the Arab military who were their true targets. The Irgun attack was, however, roundly condemned by the Jewish Agency and the Haganah. Later in 1948 the Irgun disbanded and its units merged with the new Israel Defence Forces. The Stern Gang was banned and broke up.

Whatever the truth of the Deir Yassin incident, it was perceived by the world as an atrocity. However, it struck a fatal blow at Arab attempts to thwart the foundation of the Israeli state. The Arab press itself contributed to this, by playing up the story. Its intention was to damage the image of the Yishuv – the Palestine Jews – but the effect was to terrify and demoralise Palestine Arabs. The name of the Irgun now struck terror even in the hearts of Arab soldiers. Only a month after the massacre, at least 300,000 Palestine Arabs had fled the country, though in the hope of returning soon in the wake of vengeful and conquering Arab armies. Arabs who elected to stay moved away from centres of concentrated Jewish population. Jewish authority was now unquestioned both on the coastal plain and in western Galilee. Whatever shape or form the final Jewish state would have, these areas would be part of it.

The Arabs hit back within weeks of Deir Yassin. Terrorists ambushed a medical convoy on its way to the Hadassah Hospital and the Hebrew University on the relatively isolated Mount Scopus, and killed seventy-seven doctors, nurses, students and lecturers. One of the nastiest aspects of this attack, which lasted seven hours, is that it occurred within 200 yards of a British military post whose soldiers took no action at all. Among the dead was the fiancé of Ben-Gurion's daughter Renana.

The Arab migration following Deir Yassin had grave consequences for the population of Haifa. At the time, some 60,000 Arabs and 60,000 Jews lived in the town. They ran the town council jointly, and if any one place could demonstrate that it was possible for the two groups to prosper and live in peace side by side, Haifa was it. Unfortunately the two terrorist actions dealt a major blow to the two communities. Fearing further violence, nervous Arabs began planning to leave the city. As bloody reprisals and counter-reprisals followed the Deir Yassin and the Mount Scopus atrocities, the British commander in Haifa, Major-General Stockwell, in an effort to avert this exodus, arranged a meeting with the Arab leaders in the city to inform them that the Haganah had prepared armistice terms. The Jewish mayor also appealed to the Arabs to stay.

The Arab delegation, consisting of two Muslims and four Christians, asked for time to contact the Arab states to sound them out about the situation. They returned that evening with disappointing news. There could be no question of signing any document of any kind, and furthermore, Arabs wishing to leave Haifa could do so with the blessing of the Arab states, who would provide refuge for them if they wished. There was something in this which indicated the intervention of the Mufti, in exile in Egypt. The Mufti also had *agents provocateurs* in place in Haifa.

Stockwell could not believe his ears, and the mayor, who had made many close friends in the Arab community over the years, began to weep. In an effort to resolve the situation, Archbishop Hakim and two other Arab leaders left for Egypt in the hope of persuading the Mufti at least to withdraw his followers from Haifa.

Predictably, this the Mufti refused to do, and soon afterwards Arab radio stations outside Palestine started to broadcast threats of punishment to those Arabs who elected to stay in Haifa. Despite the pleas of well-meaning British and Jewish friends and colleagues, most of the Arab community now began to pack their bags.

The country was in ferment, and the departure of the British was only weeks away.

Chapter Twenty-Five:
Mounting Pressure

Pressure on Ben-Gurion mounted steadily during the early part of 1948. The problems faced by the Jews of Palestine indicated that, surely, the country was in no position to proclaim itself a sovereign state. The idea was still wonderful, but was this the time? Wouldn't it be more prudent to wait?

Zionist leaders from America flew in early in the year, and after meetings with their Palestinian counterparts they felt that the step Ben-Gurion was proposing was not only too radical, but risked putting the whole idea of a Jewish homeland out of reach forever. The fact had to be faced that the nascent Jewish army was no match for the combined Arab states which surrounded the country. Ben-Gurion considered his position to be like Churchill's in 1940: he stood alone.

But, like Churchill, he was not quite alone. He managed to persuade his people to stand by him, and he sent Golda Meir, an ally from the early days, to the United States to canvass for money from American Jewry to buy badly needed arms for his soldiers.

Everything at that time was moving fast, and no sooner had the decision been made to send Mrs Meir than she was on a plane. She travelled without luggage, pausing only to throw on a winter coat over the clothes she was wearing, and she went unannounced and unrehearsed to ask people who had never heard of her to give money to a cause that was perhaps not at the forefront of most of their minds. Her first port of call was Chicago, and on 21 January, at the General Assembly of the Council of Jewish Federation and Welfare Funds, she stood to face a meeting of professional fundraisers. Her arrival had been so sudden that she was not even on the list of speakers. It was small wonder that a few of them settled back to listen with a certain amount of scepticism.

Within minutes, however, Golda Meir had this tough crowd of Jewish Americans on the edges of their seats. She described the situation in Palestine as only someone who was living through it herself could. She was not there, she told them, to plead for a few hundred thousand Jews in Palestine alone. It would, she said, "be audacity on our part to worry Jews throughout the world because a few thousand more Jews are in danger". But she echoed Churchill's combative words of the war years when she added, her voice ringing round the room, that the Jews of Palestine would "fight in the Negev and fight in Galilee and fight on the outskirts of Jerusalem until the very end".

Though a short one, the speech was electrifying. Many of those who listened were moved to tears, and when Golda had finished the people in the room rose as one to cheer her. More importantly, they agreed to pledge money for the cause in amounts that she could scarcely have dreamt of. For six weeks she toured the USA, and for six weeks her listeners wept and gave money – many taking out bank loans to do so, so determined were they to help in the struggle of the Jews of Palestine.

Meanwhile, as we have seen, the situation in Palestine continued to be tense as terrorist attacks continued. The Haganah counted a mere 20,000 partially trained men and women, and there were not enough weapons to go round even this small force. As for aeroplanes, all they had was a handful of Piper Cubs. The one military group which was undeniably ready for combat was the Palmach. This extremely well-trained strike force now consisted of 3,000 men and 1,000 women. Many of them were World War Two veterans who had fought alongside the British as commandos. The Palmach units had their bases at key border positions, well away from the risk of interference from the British.

The Palmach would form the backbone of the Jewish struggle, but there was no lack of young people eager to defend their homeland, and the Jewish Agency announced conscription for all men and women aged between seventeen and twenty-five. By then it was possible to travel from city to city only in armed convoys, and the main road linking Jerusalem and Tel Aviv was a favourite target for raiding Arabs.

Naturally this made communications difficult and sometimes impossible – a fact which caused grave concern to Haim Cohen, who with his team had now completed the new legislation, ready for Ben-Gurion's inspection:

> You have to remember that we were in a state of siege. It was almost impossible to travel, and there were no telephones working. In Jerusalem we were entirely cut off. And yet I had to get the documents to Tel Aviv.
>
> On 5 May, scarcely more than a week before the new state was to be declared, I was without orders. The Jerusalem committee decided that I would have to take the documents to Tel Aviv personally. Before I left, just in case, I opened the folder marked COURT OF JUSTICE and I began to appoint prosecutors and judges and clerks and so forth, so that everything would be set up and ready to go into operation. Then I made a quick speech on behalf of the Secretary of State, though I had no idea who this might be; later on I found that the actual appointment wasn't Secretary of State at all, but Justice Minister.
>
> There remained the problem of how to get to Tel Aviv. We tracked down a radio to see if we could make contact with our people there, but we had no transmitter. Then the Minister sent me a message to the effect that the army would escort me to Tel Aviv; but when I made contact with their transport office, and told them why I needed the escort, they replied that they had higher transport priorities than getting the new laws from Jerusalem to Tel Aviv. Truly it was chaos.
>
> I had to wait two weeks in the end; and then they found me a jeep to take me part of the way only. The whole journey took fourteen hours and I made it partly in the jeep, partly on foot and partly by bus. What's more, the Jerusalem Post Office had saddled me

with a huge sack of letters for Tel Aviv which they had no other means of delivering! I remember that when I got to Tel Aviv the most important thing for me was not delivering the new laws to Ben-Gurion, but getting rid of that sack. And I was never paid, either for drafting the legislation or delivering the post!

In early 1948, Yehuda Ariel was a unit commander with the Haganah. He was responsible not only for getting immigrants and arms into the country, but for finding places of relative safety for the immigrants to settle:

One night we brought in about thirty boys and girls, and with the help of another hundred people we managed to erect six small settlements despite the curfew. Usually, we'd get notice of the arrival of immigrants about three days before they came. I gave orders to shoot on sight any British soldiers who tried to intervene. Our weapons were ones which we'd stolen from British camps.

We'd erected some tents and makeshift cabins which the British told us to dismantle; but we were able to cite an old law from the time of the Turkish rule which hadn't been repealed, which stated that once there is a roof on a structure, it cannot be touched. The British were furious, but there was nothing they could do. Actually only the officer was really angry; the men sat down with us and had some tea and toast and marmalade. They were just young soldiers, the same age as we were, and they could see how tough things were for us. I remember how cold it was, and how we danced to forget our hunger. We didn't even have much water, and what we had we had to carry in containers from the valley near the Sea of Galilee up to our settlement on the mountainside. The latrines were set up a good way outside the stockade, which meant that relieving yourself was always a dangerous operation. We never went alone and we always went armed.

If Arab forces were ever able to take a kibbutz, they destroyed it. Yochanan Dreyfus entered one which had been in Syrian hands for just two days:

During that time they had destroyed everything. All the wood had been torn out and burnt – the door frames, the windows, the roof, everything. It took us three months to rebuild the place, and it was cold and wet at the time.

Spring seemed far away.

Chapter Twenty-Six: Day of Freedom

In the last few days of British rule, while Ben-Gurion struggled with the text of the proclamation of the new state and wondered if he would in fact ever be reading it out, several commanders of the Haganah in Tel Aviv made their way to the "red house" – an unimposing building painted a dull shade of pink, which was their secret HQ. On three sides of their country, Arab armies were mobilising. On the fourth, the Mediterranean carried in ships bearing arms and immigrants; but it also carried the British warships which still sought to prevent both from coming in.

Guns and planes were needed desperately. There was an abundance of military surplus available in Europe and to be had cheaply after the end of the Second World War; and thanks to their American friends the Jews of Palestine had been given the means to buy what they needed; but still there was the problem of getting the equipment in. And time was passing ever more quickly. There were warplanes ready and waiting – ten fighters in Czechoslovakia (ironically the first four fighters actually to be flown by Israel were Messerschmitts); bombers and crews standing by elsewhere; but the ships that were bringing supplies across the Mediterranean were too slow.

Aeroplanes were the answer; but then there was the question of refuelling. Feelers had been put out to countries like Italy to grant landing permission; but British pressure there had once again stymied any hope of co-operation; and the same went for Greece, which had its own problems at the time. The only aircraft with a long enough range to be useful without depending on refuelling facilities were four Constellations, and they were grounded in Panama and in the USA – thousands of miles from where they were needed.

There was one small piece of good news for the embattled Yishuv: a ship called the *Bora* was approaching Tel Aviv with a cargo of onions, potatoes and tomato juice. The Haganah knew that she was also secretly carrying five 65-mm field-guns, and a consignment of light rifles and French machine-guns, together with three million rounds of ammunition.

The *Bora* made her way slowly to a point off Tel Aviv and dropped anchor. As she did so, two Royal Navy destroyers arrived to check her papers and bills of lading. The forged documents appeared to satisfy the British officers, but the destroyers refused to move off. From the shore, Ben-Gurion and his military aides watched the situation anxiously through binoculars. So desperate were they to get the arms ashore that one suggested blowing the ship up in the hope that the cargo would drift inshore with the wreckage, where it could be salvaged.

But such drastic measures were not needed. As the *Bora* steamed slowly northwards towards the harbour at Haifa that night, her escort left her. Soon, she would be unloading her much-needed cargo for the defence of the new country – for the next day was 14 May, Independence Day.

The day itself was marred by a disastrous attack on Tel Aviv Airport by two Egyptian Spitfires, which flew in from the sea at 1,000 feet and riddled the small planes on the ground with bullets. A machine-gun brought one of the Spitfires down, however, as its pilot was forced to crash-land on the beach. Ben-Gurion had no reason to rejoice for the new state he had declared. He said himself that he felt "no gaiety in me, only deep anxiety" and also, "If we were [now] responsible for our destiny, the rational question might well be whether in a few days or a few weeks we would have a destiny to shape."

However, with the departure of the British, all restrictions on incoming arms and people were finally lifted completely and, just as idealists had gone to fight in Spain against Franco a decade or so earlier, so now Jews from all over the Diaspora made their way to swell the ranks of the armed forces of Israel. There was no need for complete despondency. The British Foreign Secretary had warned Transjordan not to invade the territory allocated to the Jews, and although the ratio of the local Arab populations to the Jewish population was overwhelming – forty to one – in terms of engaged forces the two sides were roughly equal. And although the Arabs initially had vastly superior weaponry and the advantage of air cover, the Jews had better morale and greater initiative. Above all, perhaps, theirs was to be a co-ordinated campaign.

The mood of the country on Independence Day was captured by Professor Even-Paz, who with his family were arriving as immigrants:

> We heard the announcement on the radio on the evening of the 14th. The state had been declared and the British would be leaving the following day. On board, the ship's nurse had spent a whole night making a flag, so that when we steamed into port we were the first vessel to enter it with the Jewish flag flying.
>
> When we arrived in Tel Aviv the first thing we saw was two Egyptian planes shooting up the aerodrome. Our people hustled us off the boat, and we had to abandon our luggage – which didn't bother us too much since it only consisted of a rucksack. We went through customs, which was already organised with Jewish officials there. They greeted us with a bag of fruit and a bag of sweets. Then we all got on to buses. I carried my little girl in my arms.
>
> We started to drive off, but we were stopped every so often by people throwing sweets into the bus and shouting, "Welcome!" They thought we were from Cyprus and kept asking if we knew so-and-so or had seen so-and-so. Even after we'd left Tel Aviv we were still stopped on the open road.

Rina Agagin was sitting with her family by her radio in Baghdad when she heard the news of the Proclamation of Independence:

> We'd known it was coming because we'd heard about the vote in the UN, and we also got news from the underground Zionist emissaries who used to brief us regularly.

Everything the Jewish community in Baghdad did was secretive. We used to meet in secret to learn Hebrew and to learn about Zionism. Sadly for me, only children over fourteen years old were allowed because they couldn't take a chance with the younger ones. I was under fourteen then, so I couldn't attend the meetings or learn Hebrew.

On the night of the Declaration – it was a Friday night – we all dressed up and we made a special *kiddush* [blessing prayer] as they'd told us on leaflets that had already been distributed. How we celebrated!

Sam Bresler had made his way to Tel Aviv from his unit to be present at the moment when history was made:

There was a huge crowd in the street and I was with them. Ben-Gurion came out on to the balcony. Everybody was singing and dancing, and when he read the announcement people started to cry.

One of the first soldiers to be created an officer in the new state was Captain David Shenhabi. He was stationed in the headquarters of the provisional government. Hardly had the Proclamation left Ben-Gurion's lips than David set off to visit a friend:

On the way we bought a bottle of champagne. That night we sat around the radio and we didn't stop dancing. We danced in the flat, and when we got fed up with that, we went and danced in the street!

As the departing British High Commissioner, Sir Alan Cunningham, boarded the cruiser HMS *Euryalus*, the Arab states mobilised. King Abdullah ibn Hussein of Transjordan had already signalled his intention to the Arab League of entering Palestine the moment the British Mandate came to an end. Not all the member states of the League were as keen to fight as Abdullah, but all were drawn into the war. President Truman, despite recent wavering, recognised the new state of Israel within twenty-four hours of its having been proclaimed, and the USSR followed within days; but such political gestures cut no ice with the Arabs, and in Britain both the Foreign Office and the Chiefs of Staff were convinced that the Arabs would quickly throw the Yishuv into the Mediterranean.

Nevertheless, Truman's imprimatur was the signal for further rejoicing in Israel, and as several smaller countries followed the USA's lead, what had been a dream for so long seemed confirmed as reality.

But there was no time to rest. Ben-Gurion broadcast to the world news of the struggle that now faced Israel. No sooner had he finished than the airport was hit by another attack, this time by bombers. As Ben-Gurion drove at sunrise through the streets of Tel Aviv, memories of the Blitz in London came back to him. Bombing on a much larger scale had had no effect on the will of the British people to defeat Nazism. He was certain that the Jews of Palestine, who had already endured so much, would be equally resolute in withstanding whatever it was the Arab nations could throw at them.

Chapter Twenty-Seven:
The Battle Begins

The Egyptian Army struck in the south and advanced swiftly through the undefended Negev Desert. Settlements in its path were overrun as the Arabs made their way north. Those villages and towns that were without anti-aircraft weapons were defenceless against strikes by Spitfires of the Egyptian Air Force.

The Syrians and the Lebanese attacked from the north as units of the Iraqi Army and the Arab Legion swept into the country from the east. Although their attack was not as well co-ordinated as that which had been planned by the Arab Chiefs of Staff in Damascus, they were nevertheless convinced that the tiny new country would be powerless to withstand the might of the joint forces now descending on it. Abdur-Raham Azzam Pasha, the Secretary-General of the Arab League, declared to the world's assembled media that "this would be a war of extermination and a momentous massacre which will be spoken of like the Mongolian massacres and the Crusades".

The Jews had won the battle to be recognised. Now they had to fight to hold on to their political gains. The forces of the Haganah had been swelled already by the influx of volunteers from overseas. Ben Ocopnick from Canada, who, it will be remembered, had been sent back after his first trip to Palestine to recruit for the Defence Forces, now returned to help Eretz Israël even before the new state had been officially proclaimed; and he was not short of company:

After about three or four weeks of training we were so short of ammunition that we only had six rounds per man. We were a real mixed bag and we fought as regular infantry or as commandos according to what was needed. For a time I even served on the first Israeli warship, the *Wedgwood*; and for a time, too, I ran the airstrip in Beersheba. We got paid next to nothing – about $20 a month. The most important thing was our cigarettes. I remember once we all refused to fight because we hadn't had our issue!

I wasn't the only one fighting for what we believed in. I think altogether there were about 200 Canadians in Palestine at the time. And there were at least 500 Americans. We were already fighting the Arabs when the state was proclaimed, and frankly we were just too busy fighting to care. At night we'd harass their lines and by day they'd try to get up to the hills to flush us out.

It's very difficult now to look back and take a perspective on the positive things. I remember the fear we felt every waking minute, and I remember going into action feeling panic-stricken as we passed the ambulances and the stretcher-bearers coming back from the front with the wounded. There always seemed to be an impossible number of wounded. We were lucky; we had an experienced soldier on our team called Jules Lewis. He'd been a sergeant in the Canadian Army and he'd been decorated. He knew what to do, and he kept us alive.

We fought hard and we fought well. All of us were scared – anyone who isn't frightened in battle is an idiot! But we did our job, and we did it properly. Our commanders were Palestine Jews, but we also had liaison officers to translate orders when it was necessary; and we had other men besides Lewis who'd had experience of war. Our own commander came from Halifax, Nova Scotia, and he was pretty good. Then there was an uncle of mine who'd fought in the Spanish Civil War, and also in a couple of uprisings in South America.

He used to run into position, firing or being fired on, and then he'd make his way from dugout to dugout to make sure we were all right. When he got to me he'd lie down next to me and say, "How're you doing, Benny?" I'd say, "Fine." He'd then say, "Don't worry, we'll be back in camp in an hour or two. We're doing a good job; we'll clean them out."

On the actual day of the proclamation we were up in the hills, just outside Jerusalem, keeping some Arabs pinned down in their villages so they couldn't come out and attack the town. We were running out of water and ammunition, and four or five of the guys volunteered to go and fetch fresh supplies. They left at dusk, and when they returned the next day, they told us the news: "We just heard that Ben-Gurion declared the Jewish State. Isn't that terrific?" We said, "Terrific. But when the hell do we get the hell out of here?"

We'd been up there four days and nights, and we were getting a little fed up with being sort of trapped in that position. But we finally got out the next day.

Leslie Read from England was assigned to a military camp near Haifa. He had a letter of introduction to a family in the town from a university friend:

I was lucky to have this family to visit. Our pay was terrible: a few pounds a month and three or four packets of cigarettes a week.

I was eventually put into a unit called the Anglo-Saxon Brigade. We never learnt Hebrew but used English. The sergeant was a Canadian, the lieutenant was South African and the captain was American. All three were Gentiles, and I think they were all soldiers of fortune. We stood by and were sent into action wherever we were needed. It was a most peculiar war. We would fight for three or four days, and then the UN would intervene and there would be a truce, so that we'd just sit, looking at one another across no-man's-land. They tried to give us some training, but it didn't amount to much, and we didn't have enough weapons; though I do remember two tanks, stolen from the British. A friend of mine had been a tank commander and he used to take these tanks into action, use them hard, then pull them out quickly. Then they'd be taken on transporters to another part of the country, where they would put them into action again. This was a ploy to make the Arabs think we had far more tanks than we did.

I became a machine-gunner. My gun was a German weapon and it was very good indeed: it was really something, to be using a German gun to fight for the Jewish state! I fought until the end of 1948 when I was wounded in the head. I was discharged from the army and they shipped me home.

On the day of the proclamation, the Egyptians attacked Yad Mordechai kibbutz from the air. This kibbutz of Polish veterans had been named after Mordechai Ancelewicz, one of the leaders of the Warsaw Ghetto uprising. It lay on the Gaza-Jerusalem highway and, like many of the isolated settlements, it had until recently been on friendly terms with its Arab neighbours. The attacks lasted several days, during which the kibbutz, representing many years of hard work, was destroyed and twenty-seven settlers were killed. Other kibbutzim met a similar fate during the war, as Yaakov Edelstein remembers:

> Our kibbutz was under siege for six months. Then the Arabs launched a final mass attack and they managed to overrun the place. I was on guard duty at the time. I knew that this was the end, and that there was no chance either to escape or save the kibbutz. Our commanders told us to retreat to the centre of the settlement and raise our hands above our heads in surrender. We laid down our guns and obeyed. They were trying to save our lives. There were about forty of us.
>
> When the Arabs came up, they just started shooting at us immediately. We were defenceless, Most of us were injured on the spot, but a handful of people including myself were not hit and we managed to run into the fields to hide. An elderly Arab discovered us there, but he took us under his protection and saved us from the mob until he was able to hand us over to some soldiers from the Arab Legion. They told us they would send us back to Transjordan to their king, Abdullah, and there we joined 700 other Jewish prisoners-of-war. We were beaten and starved, but after a Red Cross delegation arrived, our conditions improved. Even so, we were in constant fear of being killed.
>
> They kept us in a camp near the Iraqi border for a year. It was a very primitive place, but they didn't treat us badly there. In the end, there was an exchange of prisoners and we were returned to Israel.

News coming in from the various fronts to Tel Aviv was not good. The Arab Legion had overrun some small settlements to the north and south of Jerusalem before attacking the city itself. By the end of the first three weeks of the war, Jerusalem had been hit by over 3,000 shells, and almost 100,000 Jews were cut off in the New City, starving and without water. The Israeli garrison

in the Old City held out until 28 May, when it surrendered to
the Arab Legion. The following day, however, the UN Security
Council called for a truce, which was implemented on 11 June
and held for a month. All that, however, was still some way
in the future, and I will return to it.

Meanwhile, in the south of the country, Negev settlements
were under attack from Egyptian, Sudanese, Saudi Arabian
and Yemeni forces. It was clear that they meant to push up
as far as Beersheba and then turn towards Jerusalem to join
forces with the Arab Legion in an attempt to sequester the
city, while another army would go up the coast to Tel Aviv,
to meet the armies of Syria, Iraq and the Lebanon which were
active in Galilee.

But however confident the Arab offensive was, and however
much the Arab propaganda machine predicted a swift end to
hostilities with the final removal of every Jew from the soil of
Palestine, the Arab League reckoned without the iron determination of the Yishuv to hang on to what they had got. The Jews
of Palestine might have been outnumbered; they were certainly
outgunned; but they were fighting for their homeland and they
were infused with a spirit which was impossible to overcome.
Throughout the country, settlements, although separated from
one another sometimes by miles of desert, were resolved to
hold on to what they had struggled to produce. From holes
dug in the ground they mounted primitive, home-made guns
and mortars, and raked the enemy as they strove to keep the
road linking Tel Aviv to the Negev open.

In the end, of forty major settlements throughout the country,
only two would fall. Soon, the Egyptian forces in the south would
find themselves brought to a virtual standstill; while in the north,
the Syrians were faring no better. They were turned back at
the settlements of Degania, among whose defenders was the
young Moshe Dayan, as early as 20 May; and by the 23rd
they had left the Jordan valley. Although the following day
saw the evacuation of the kibbutz Yad Mordechai, the Jews
were greatly encouraged at their unhoped-for victories, and
every day that they succeeded in holding the Arabs in check
made them stronger, for now weapons were pouring into the
country through the ports.

David Shenhabi was heading south with his troops to confront the Egyptian army which was pushing up the coast towards Tel Aviv:

> The Egyptians had everything. Armour, aircraft, the lot. Those who tell you that they were never afraid are lying, though if you are in the middle of a battle, and especially if you are a commander, you don't have the time to think about fear: you're too busy, and you work like a machine.
>
> My soldiers were all people who had only had a few hours' spare-time training. After the first UN cease-fire was called, we found that we had sustained a large number of casualties, but we kept taking the immigrants off the ships as they came in, trained them fast and used them to fill the ranks. It was tough for them; they had only just arrived; but the ones who came from internment in Cyprus were fantastic: idealistic and energetic young people.

What the Arabs lacked were moral conviction and proper co-ordination, and these were crucial. In some ways it is hard to see how they could lose otherwise, since apart from superior arms, they had other advantages: they controlled the strategically superior hilly regions of Palestine and could draw on almost limitless manpower. Supply lines were no problem and the Arab Legion, the best of all the armies, had all but taken the psychologically vital city of Jerusalem.

The Israelis started with an air force of nine fighters, of which only one was twin-engined; their arms, as we have seen, were laughable, though they would improve after the British had left. The ranks of the Haganah had grown to 45,000, however, and also incorporated a few thousand members of the old Irgun and Stern organisations. Combing every pocket of the Jewish population, Ben-Gurion came up with another 13,500 people or so from the kibbutzim and the moshavim (workers' settlements) with combat experience. Out of all these groups the Israel Defence Forces were born.

There was more work to be done on the civil infrastructure of the new state. The departing British had run down certain services some time before leaving – taxes had not been collected and health care had been neglected. There was a need for experienced civil servants to come and sort out the mess. Ben-Gurion appealed to friendly governments overseas to help by sending such people to Israel. Few individuals wished to respond.

If foreign help in this area was not forthcoming, then at least there were capable people at home who could take up the reins and learn as they drove. Haim Cohen, who had done such masterly work in preparing the new legislation, now found himself catapulted into public office:

> I was summoned to Tel Aviv to continue what I had started. There, I met an old friend and colleague who told me that I was to be appointed Director of Legislation. That was my first official title, and I was given a tiny office with a table and chair.
>
> I'd been Director of Legislation for just under a week when I was told that Ben-Gurion wanted to see me. As soon as I met him again he said, "I hear you're a good lawyer." I agreed. He said, "Yes, you've had a lot of success in the courts. So, from tomorrow, consider yourself appointed Public Prosecutor."
>
> I told him that I had never been a prosecutor and that I knew nothing about the job. He leant across his desk and looked me in the eye. "Every soldier in this country as well as everyone else has to obey orders. I order you to become Public Prosecutor." So, the next day I duly started work as Public Prosecutor.

Ben-Gurion also introduced changes in the new armed forces, replacing old-guard commanders with new blood. The thirty-three-year-old Moshe Dayan, a former member of the Palmach, for example, was made Military Commander of Jerusalem.

Ben-Gurion appointed himself overall commander of the armed forces, though this did cause raised eyebrows. What did the Prime Minister know of military logistics? Ben-Gurion swept objections aside. This was not a time to hesitate and cavil; what was needed was a man of decision, and he was that man.

And as the war went on, Israel became more confident, because arms and new citizens continued to flow in daily through the gates which the British had kept closed for so long, but which Ben-Gurion had now flung wide open.

Chapter Twenty-Eight:
Divided Loyalties

Israel continued to be supported by friends from abroad. Ben Dunkelman fought so bravely that a bridge he held successfully still bears his name. The Jewish American Colonel David "Mickey" Marcus undertook the work of pulling together the nascent Israeli Army – though he was tragically to be shot by one of his own men who mistook him for an Arab soldier in the dark.

One of those who should have been with the first group of Canadians to leave was Joe Warner. In fact he didn't leave Canada until after Passover in 1948:

I delayed because I thought it would upset my family even more if I wasn't there for *Pesach*, so I volunteered to leave with the second group, which left immediately afterwards.

We travelled from Toronto to New York by train. Some of the boys had problems getting across the border because the Americans were suspicious of people of military age – I think they knew what we were up to. We spent five or six days in New York before boarding a Polish liner called the SS *Sobieski*.

We sailed via Gibraltar and left the ship at Cannes. There we were met by a member of the Haganah who took us to a camp near Marseilles called G.

Our passports were taken away from us and we were told that we'd be leaving for Palestine on a Romanian ship called the *Transylvania*, but a couple of days before we were due to set off news came through that Lloyd's of London had designated Palestine waters as "war waters", and they would not cover any damage to the ship, with the result that her owners backed out of sailing her. Instead of leaving, we were sent to a mountain retreat above Marseilles called Ste Thérèse, and there we spent a couple of weeks waiting for alternative transport.

During that time we did whatever training we could to keep in shape, but of course we had no weapons. Eventually they bussed us to a little port near Marseilles called La Ciotat, and put us on a fishing boat which had just returned from the Grand Banks. I can still smell the fish!

There were over 200 of us on that ship, and there was only one lifeboat, which had a hole in it big enough to put your head through. We had a very hairy trip, but in the end we got to Herzliyya Petuach. There we were met and given a bun and an orange, and then we were sent on to a camp at Hadera, where we mingled with the concentration camp survivors and other displaced persons: we were illegal immigrants – neither the British nor the UN were keen to see able-bodied young men coming into the country at that time; not that anyone could have averted war, by any measures, then.

The camp was full of volunteers – Americans, British, Canadians, and even some Belgians. Pretty soon recruitment officers came from the Army and the Navy; but I told them I was hoping to join the Air Force. I'd been a wireless operator/gunner in the Royal Canadian Air Force during the war.

There was no one from that branch of the services, so I left the camp and went to Tel Aviv where the Air Force had its HQ; but the Air Force scarcely existed at that time and they had nothing for me. They said however that they'd put me up at a hotel on the beach until I was needed.

After a few days of twiddling my thumbs I got fed up – I hadn't come to Israel to sit by the sea while there was a war going on. I went back to Air Force HQ and told them that I'd decided to join the Army, but that I would keep them informed of my whereabouts so that they could still call on me as soon as I was needed. Then I went to a place just north of Petach Tikvah to join a mortar unit supporting the infantry.

I'll never forget the first battle, soon after the British had left. There were Arab snipers in the hill villages overlooking the Haifa road. Haifa was the only outlet to the world outside and it was vital that the road remain open.

It was a very primitive operation; we had very poor equipment and there was a shortage of guns and ammunition, but that's where we did our first fighting. After that action, we were turned into an anti-tank unit and sent to a big camp south of Tel Aviv, where we joined up with the famous Givati Infantry Brigade. They gave us an anti-tank gun which they'd captured from the Egyptians and a British six-pounder. We fought in battles around places like Qiryat Gat – all the areas which opened the roads going to the Negev.

After a year of it, I began to feel that it was time to return to Canada. I had just turned twenty-three; for me I felt that the fighting was over, and I wanted to complete my education. But then one day my commanding officer asked me to set up a first-aid station. I went around scrounging supplies wherever I could, and finally found myself at a big warehouse full of captured Egyptian medical equipment. The warehouse was run by a young Army girl who was very helpful, and gave me all kinds of bandages, plasters, ampoules of morphine and so forth.

One day she asked me if I'd like to go to a party in Tel Aviv with her – a friend of hers was getting engaged. Well, I went along, and soon afterwards I was engaged myself! I've been married to that Army girl now for forty-five years, and we have two fabulous sons, both born in Israel.

As the war dragged on, so cracks began to appear in the unity of the Israelis. There were still those among the military commanders who doubted Ben-Gurion's ability as a generalissimo, and some who resented his political absolutism. Among them was Israel Galili, a commander who had helped form the Palmach, and even in the party which Ben-Gurion had founded, the socialist MAPAI, there were dissident voices. Ben-Gurion suspected that his appointee, "Mickey" Marcus, had not been killed by accident at all; but an investigation came to nothing. Privately, Ben-Gurion remained unsatisfied.

He had already had to cope with the extreme right of the Irgun, which had opposed his authority from the start and was reluctant to see any of its group subsumed within the

Israel Defence Forces. This was a battle which Ben-Gurion would win; but he and Menachem Begin were political enemies ever afterwards, and Ben-Gurion made a point of meeting the extremist leader, whom he regarded as a would-be dictator, only when it was absolutely necessary.

The rift with the Irgun was to have very serious consequences. On 28 May 1948, Order Number Four of Ben-Gurion's Provisional Government ratified the creation of the Israel Defence Forces. The following day, as the UN Security Council called for the truce, the first four Messerschmitt fighters of the Israeli Air Force attacked an Egyptian column heading north towards Tel Aviv, bringing it to a halt and challenging Egyptian air dominance.

The Irgun, however, was still an independent force to be reckoned with, and Ben-Gurion was aware of Begin's own ambitions. The UN truce was, as we have seen, brought into force on 11 June. A week later, Ben-Gurion had the chance to show Begin who was boss.

Chapter Twenty-Nine: Uneasy Peace

The *Altalena* set sail from the French town of Port-de-Bouc carrying a huge supply of arms – enough to equip ten battalions – and nearly 1,000 Jewish immigrants. The arms were apparently a gift of the French government in acknowledgement of France's sympathy for Israel in her struggle for independence (France was having her own problems with Arabs fighting for their independence in North Africa, so it was also good to keep the Arabs of the Middle East tied up with Israel). The voyage had been given a lot of publicity, and both the armaments and the volunteers were badly needed; but there were two problems. The first was that both passengers and arms were destined not for Ben-Gurion's partially formed official forces, but for Begin's Irgun (though Begin said that he would insist on only twenty of the weapons). The second was that the shipment of so great a consignment of arms and – effectively – troops into the country during the UN truce would constitute a breach of the Security Council ruling on the truce.

There was a third unspoken problem: with such great reinforcements, Begin might be in a position to challenge the authority of Ben-Gurion's Provisional Government.

Ben-Gurion was determined to nip any such threat in the bud. On 21 June he gave the order for the Israel Defence Forces (but effectively the élite Palmach) to set the *Altalena* on fire by shelling her as she lay just off Tel Aviv. In the fighting during the action, fifteen people were killed, mainly members of the Irgun. Most of those on board had managed to land safely.

Civil war seemed very close, but then Begin, who had been aboard at the time of the fighting, broadcast a statement to the effect that "Irgun soldiers will not be a party to fratricidal warfare; but nor will they accept the discipline of Ben-Gurion's army any longer. Within the state area we will continue our political activities; our fighting strength we will conserve for the enemy outside." It may be that by this show of "moderation", Begin sought to cast Ben-Gurion in the role of villain and gain a moral if not a political victory. In the latter sense at least he did not succeed, and Ben-Gurion, who in any case was bound to accept his statement in order to defuse the situation, remained in power. But the *Altalena* episode preoccupied political discussion for a very long time afterwards.

David Gen, a former US merchant navy officer, was on board the *Altalena* when it was attacked:

I was among those who arranged the purchase of the ship, which we had refurbished at Staten Island. Meanwhile, the Irgun made contact with a member of the Socialist Party in France. They, the French, agreed to supply the Irgun with 4,000 tons of arms; more than Israel had already in the whole of the country. I suppose the French did it because they were against the British. When we began loading the arms there was co-operation between the three groups, Irgun, Palmach and Haganah – a co-operation which would not last.

Anyway, we began to load the arms, and, in addition, 934 passengers, and we set sail from Port-de-Bouc, west of Marseilles. It was well after the Proclamation of Independence, so there was no problem with the British and we arrived safely off the coast of Israel on 19 June 1948. Our one problem was that we didn't have radio contact with Israel. We could hear them but they couldn't hear us.

When Ben-Gurion heard the news that an incredible number of arms was on its way under the control of the Irgun he became very uneasy, concerned that there might be a *coup d'état*. He gave orders that the ship was not to dock. This made it difficult for us. We were over halfway there and we couldn't go back. We had over 900 people on board and we were running out of water, so we decided to carry on. As we lay offshore we were told over the radio to make for Kfar Vitkin, a left-wing kibbutz south of Haifa. We couldn't find it at first and it wasn't marked on the charts, but after some confusion – we had to drop anchor and send a Hebrew-speaking crew member ashore in one of the boats to ask where the place was – we reached it: they lit up the beach with car headlights for us. We dropped anchor again at four o'clock on the Saturday morning. Then those ashore came out to us in small boats and started to unload our passengers.

We also started to unload the cargo of arms, but then there was trouble on shore. The Palmach, under orders from Ben-Gurion, arrived to stop us. By late afternoon the situation between Palmach and Irgun was very tense.

By that time Menachem Begin had arrived on the scene. As head of the Irgun he was more anxious than most to make sure the arms came ashore. He made his way on to the ship and joined the crew in their efforts. Suddenly, shooting started on shore between the Irgun and the Palmach. We stopped unloading and decided to get under way because we were afraid that mortar fire from the shore would hit the ship and blow us up. But because the road was higher than the port, their shells were going over our heads.

We decided to make a run for Tel Aviv, though by now we had an Israeli naval ship in pursuit, which was firing at us. We had started in the late afternoon and we sailed all night, hugging the coast. Begin's hope was that we would be able to continue unloading without difficulty in Tel Aviv. We reached there early the next morning, but once again fighting broke out between Irgun and Palmach forces.

By then Begin was screaming over a loudspeaker to those on shore that we came in peace. We even hoisted the Israeli flag. It made little difference. By late afternoon they started shelling us. My belief is that neither side knew what it was doing. They were all arguing.

At about 4 p.m. Yitzhak Rabin, standing on the shore, gave the order to sink the ship. The *Altalena* caught fire with Begin, still using his loud-hailer, on the deck. I was in the engine room at the time. We were lucky that the first mortar shell hit a hold where there were uniforms, not ammunition.

The ship started to fill with smoke. A couple of the crew came down to the engine room to tell me the ship was on fire. I went up to the deck and climbed the ladder down to a small skiff, and made it to the shore. Begin refused to leave the ship and they had to carry him off, still shouting. A remarkable man. Incredible.

As we got to the shore the ship began to blow up, and finally sank.

There were other headaches facing Ben-Gurion. The UN partition plan wasn't going to work as it stood, and they sent a mediator, responsible for sorting out which parts of Palestine should now be held by Israel and which by the Arabs. The mediator appointed was the Swedish aristocrat, Count Folke Bernadotte, whose 'white buses' had, at the end of the Second World War, taken concentration camp survivors to Sweden for care and rehabilitation.

But however good his credentials – and he was ably assisted by Dr Ralph Bunche – Bernadotte's ideas for dividing up Palestine, drafted by Bunche and signed by the Count on 27 June, were not at all to the Israelis' liking. Small wonder: he proposed an alliance between Israel and Transjordan, and that King Abdullah should take over the Negev and all of Jerusalem – though the Jews would enjoy municipal autonomy there. Israel would get most of western Galilee. Haifa would be a free port and Lydda a free airport.

This plan, even though the original proposals had been toned down by Bunche, angered both sides, and both sides rejected it – the Jews because it ignored their needs, the Arabs because it was so partial to Abdullah. Ben-Gurion felt that Bernadotte, whom he didn't like personally, might as well have been acting as an agent for the British. Once again, the Israelis would have to stake their claims by force.

The truce broke down on 8 July – the day before it was due to expire anyway – and fighting lasted ten ferocious days. By the time of the second truce which ended it, the Arabs had gained nothing; but the Israelis had widened the line of communication to Jerusalem and consolidated it: from now on they would not be dislodged from the holy city. Other gains elsewhere meant that by late July more than 500,000 Arabs in all had left Israeli territory.

To finish Bernadotte's story – and it ended tragically – it is necessary to look ahead a little, to the time following the second truce. Sporadic fighting followed its declaration and lasted throughout the summer, but Bernadotte came up with a second partition proposal, again drafted by Bunche. This time Israel was to have all of western Galilee. This still didn't satisfy Israel, even though the proposal contained plans to make Jerusalem a free city.

Jerusalem had become the headquarters of the Irgun and the Stern Gang. The Sternists now decided that the time had come to assassinate Bernadotte. The same three men who had plotted the execution of Lord Moyne were responsible for the plan. One of their number was Yitzhak Shamir – although when I asked him if, as many believe, he was responsible for the assassination, he replied:

> That is not true. The group who planned to carry out the operation came to us and asked for our approval. We gave it.

Whatever the truth of the matter, the plan was communicated to the Stern commander in Jerusalem, where Bernadotte was, and just after 5 p.m. on 17 September, Bernadotte's car was ambushed and the mediator was riddled with bullets.

Ben-Gurion heard the news less than an hour later. Appalled at the damage this crime would do to Israel's standing, he ordered the dissolution of what remained of the Irgun and had a putsch launched against the Sternists. The Stern Gang, like the Irgun, was finished, though most of its leaders escaped jail and were tacitly pardoned and rehabilitated well within a year. The assassination may have been bad for Israel's image, but it had provided Ben-Gurion with the chance thoroughly to cleanse his stable, and the effect of it was to put an end to Bernadotte's unacceptable partition proposals.

Chapter Thirty:
To Open a Door to Jerusalem

The UN had not resolved the problem posed by Jerusalem. It was a holy city to all three religious groups involved. The Old City was dominated by the Arabs. The cobbled streets where the merchants plied their trade had changed little over the centuries and, long before the current tensions arose, the Jews, along with the tourists, had been the best customers of the traders here. Now, business was bad.

The Muslim district was centred on the Dome of the Rock, a magnificent building and one of the holiest mosques in the world, along with those in Mecca, Medina and Masshad. But also within the Old City was the Via Dolorosa, of central importance to Christians, and the Wailing Wall, all that remained of the Second Temple.

In a move which was as much political as symbolic, Ben-Gurion planned to move the seat of government to the New City, which lay beyond the walls of the Old and was in direct contrast to it. Here, hotels and restaurants were springing up and the streets were thronged with people dodging taxis, buses and American cars. Almost 100,000 Jews lived and worked among the tree-lined avenues, and any visitor to the suburbs would be instantly reminded of those to be found in North America.

Although nothing should be said to detract from the importance of this move, other concerns were waiting to be addressed.

The thousands pouring into the country had placed a heavy strain on the national purse-strings. Many of the new arrivals had been forced to stay in sweltering reception camps near Haifa as they anxiously waited for the government to supply them with some form of accommodation. Many of them, who had already endured the detention camps of Cyprus, were far from happy to find themselves in similar circumstances in the Promised Land, and they were impatient to settle in the prosperous towns that they had heard so much about.

As I mentioned earlier, the fighting around Jerusalem was particularly fierce, and in the battles that raged both before and between the two truces, 100,000 Jews were stranded there. Transjordanian forces crossed the Jordan over the Allenby-Bridge on 15 May and surrounded Jerusalem. When their attack on the New City was repelled on 24 May, they turned their attention to the Jewish Quarter of the Old City, and Israeli attempts to aid it came to nothing. The garrison there surrendered to the Jordanians on 28 May after receiving an undertaking from the enemy not to mistreat either the Israeli soldiers or the civilian population. This the Jordanians honoured.

However, as the war raged, the inhabitants of the New City of Jerusalem found themselves trapped in their town, with food, fuel and water rapidly running out. King Abdullah felt just as strongly about Jerusalem as Ben-Gurion, and, as we have seen, had ordered his Arab Legion to take the city. Against the advice of his generals, Ben-Gurion decided to break through the Jordanian blockade to reach his besieged countrymen.

The two opposing leaders pored over their maps, seeking a way to outflank each other in the battle for control of a city to which the UN had vainly tried to award neutral status. In this context, the word "neutral" meant nothing to either man. From the point of view of the furious Ben-Gurion in particular, there could be nothing neutral about any territory which contained Jews who were desperately seeking help.

The main difficulty facing the Jewish forces was that the road from Tel Aviv to Jerusalem was under Arab control. Charged with breaking through from the inside was my friend Ben Dunkelman, who was with a convoy trapped inside the city:

Ever since we had arrived in Jerusalem, I had been telling my colleagues that we should try to clear the Tel Aviv road; but it seemed a crazy idea to them. They thought that the defence of the city required every single man and woman we had. There was no denying that we were thinly stretched, but I continued to press for a break-out.

The conditions in the city were terrible. None of us was wearing the same uniform – we just had a collection of hand-me-downs mixed up with civilian clothing. It was hot during the day and cold at night, but because of the way the clothes were distributed some of us were comfortable during the day but frozen at night, while others were warm at night but boiled during the day. Food was running low and drinking water had to be rationed. There was no water for washing and we wore the same underwear for what seemed like an eternity.

Dunkelman went on arguing for a break-out, but the commanders in Jerusalem continued to turn him down:

It just sickened me. Jerusalem was cut off; there was almost no communication with the outside world, and we could do nothing. The only way in and out of the city was by air, and every day we'd watch as a little Auster made the daring flight from Tel Aviv and land on the roughly levelled couple of fields which served as our airstrip. The plane was used for carrying mail and for important visitors like Ben-Gurion, who came over regularly.

I met him on several occasions. I liked him, and we became pretty close friends. He seemed to go along with many of my suggestions, especially when I got the support of Yitzhak Rabin. The main idea of mine that got his backing was that we reorganise the Jerusalem Brigade on conventional lines, and use it to try to clear the road to Tel Aviv.

The date for Miriam Spielman's wedding had been changed three times because her fiancé could not get into Jerusalem and she could not get out:

It was very difficult to correspond with one another; there was no personal mail. There was also no food coming into Jerusalem. When there was finally a lull in the fighting I went to ask permission to leave Jerusalem to get married, but it was refused. In the end I made it out disguised as a soldier in an army convoy.

While Dunkelman was involved in plans to break out, Ben-Gurion was working on plans to break in. Almost from the outset of the planning sessions, however, he found himself at odds with his generals. They argued that there were other battles to be won first. Once in positions to the east of the city, they could attack the besieging legion from the rear.

Ben-Gurion wanted a frontal attack on the legion, and in the course of the argument tempers ran high; but the Prime Minister got his way. The Army would attack head-on and take the town of Latrun, thereby unlocking the door that led to Jerusalem.

Three times the Israelis threw themselves against the Arab Legion, and three times they were repulsed; but their attacks had forced the Arabs to concentrate their forces and now, before they could regroup, the Israeli Army hastily roughed out a trail which bypassed the enemy positions. The trail got the nickname of the Burma Road.

There is a story that the route was discovered by sheer chance: a jeep full of Israeli soldiers had lost its way and drove to two Arab villages close to Latrun. They immediately captured the villages and by so doing found that a hitherto unknown track led from them which skirted Latrun and picked up the route to Jerusalem beyond it. The Israelis worked frantically to carve a drivable road along this boulder-strewn mile and a half of hilly track. As soon as possible, bulldozers were brought up to clear a path for the trucks which would be needed to bring supplies from Tel Aviv; but in the meantime forty pack mules were loaded with supplies, and when the path became too hard even for them, volunteers grabbed the 40-lb sacks of flour and took over. Two hundred remarkable men, some well into their fifties, stumbled and struggled along the trail, determined to reach their embattled fellow countrymen. Six weeks later, the bulldozers had done their job and trucks were able to bring as much food and water into the New City as was needed.

By the time of the second truce – which no one believed would hold for long – much had been achieved.

Chapter Thirty-One: A Time to Talk

As the summer of 1948 came to an end, peace talks were once again under way. In terms of the land they held, the situation was still unsatisfactory to Israel: Transjordan had the Old City of Jerusalem, together with the Wailing Wall. It also held Judea and Samaria, which great bulge of country brought them to within ten miles of Tel Aviv. But the Jordanians seemed to Ben-Gurion to be the most biddable of all the Arab nations, and a permanent peace with them looked likely, given time. Besides, he had no wish to rekindle old enmities with Britain through pursuing a war with that country's favourite Arab nation.

Meanwhile the Egyptians, who were much more vehemently anti-Israeli, had begun to attack remote Negev settlements and to threaten Tel Aviv from the south. Ben-Gurion decided to use the excuse of Egyptian truce-breaking to mobilise once more and strike at their army. His action was decisive, and he drove them out of the Negev in October and December. In the latter month, he pushed on into Sinai.

Although the British offered to support Egypt, Britain's standing there had fallen, and Egypt preferred a peace deal with its unwelcome new neighbour state. The concerted Arab attempt to crush Israel had foundered. Britain gave its *de facto* recognition of Israel in January 1949.

At a ceremony to pay tribute to those who had given their

lives in the war, Ben-Gurion had difficulty in speaking as, with tears in his eyes, he told a gathering of families, "When future generations come to write the annals of Israel, they will write, not in letters of gold, but in letters of love and honour and glory; and they will list your heroic sons together with you, the fathers and mothers who raised for us, the people of Israel, such sons." He then bent to plant the first sapling of a "Defenders' Forest", to commemorate those who had lost their lives in the war.

Early in 1949 Ben-Gurion called a general election, ushering in a democratic republic governed through a one-chamber Parliament called the Knesset. There would be a President as titular head of state; but power would reside in the hands of the Prime Minister, the leader of the elected ruling party.

Democratic it certainly was. Ben-Gurion had envisaged a two-party system in which one party formed the government and the opposition kept it on course and within bounds. In fact, twenty-one parties sprang up to contest the election. All citizens over eighteen had the right to vote, regardless of race, sex or religion. When the votes were counted, Ben-Gurion and his MAPAI party were found to have won, but they had only 36 per cent of the vote. The new officially elected Prime Minister would have to rule over a ill-assorted coalition. Another struggle was about to begin.

This, however, was still a moment of triumph. The Knesset sat for the first time in February in the New City of Jerusalem. The large hall in the Jewish Agency Building had been decorated with blue and white national flags that surrounded a full-length portrait of Theodor Herzl. Of the 120 newly elected members who took their places in the hall, three were Arabs and twelve were women. Their occupations covered every aspect of Israeli life. Farmers sat beside professional politicians, writers beside bankers and mayors beside rabbis. Many of them were European Jews who had found a home in Palestine before the outbreak of the Second World War.

There was quiet in the hall as through the door walked President Chaim Weizmann, followed by a guard of honour. Everyone stood as he entered. Suddenly, the silence was pierced by the sound of the *shofar* – the ram's horn trumpet which had been used since Biblical times to herald momentous events.

Weizmann took his place on the podium and, holding his text close to his short-sighted eyes, began to read a greeting to Jewish people throughout the world. As he spoke, many of those in the hall began to weep with joy and relief. The State of Israel had entered a new phase: one in which the people would play a major role.

Epilogue

The new year also saw the peace talks with Egypt, which took place on neutral ground – on the Greek island of Rhodes, within easy reach of both sides. As the delegates took their places, observers were astonished to find that an atmosphere of friendship existed between the two parties, and as the talks progressed, the feeling that established itself was one of warmth rather than hostility. Some weeks into the talks Abdul Moneim Mustafa, the chief Egyptian political advisor, became quite ill. Amongst his sickbed visitors was Walter Eytan, the head of the Israeli delegation, who sat beside his bed and comforted him.

The armistice agreement was reached on 24 February, and it was celebrated at a party given by Ralph Bunche, for which planeloads of luxury food were flown in from Cairo. This was a magnificent start to the general negotiations with the Arab states, and similar talks led to armistices with Lebanon, Jordan and Syria by the middle of the year. Each of these agreements was recognised by the UN which, however, noted with disappointment that neither Saudi Arabia nor Iraq would come to the negotiating table.

As in all wars, there were losers: the Palestine Arabs now had no country. The end of the war had seen new lines drawn up to signify *de facto* political boundaries. We have already mentioned Transjordan's territories; Egypt now took what has become known as the Gaza Strip on the Israeli southern frontier. Despite the UN proposal that there be a new Arab state in Palestine, this was not to happen. As for Jerusalem, it had been cut in two.

Although the armistice talks on Rhodes had gone well, those going on in Lausanne in the hope of concluding permanent peace agreements were far from being settled. This conference had been set up through a UN Conciliation Committee consisting of representatives from the USA, France and Turkey. Preliminary meetings became bogged down; Israeli and Arab delegates did not meet formally, and the Arabs refused to recognise any other borders for the new state than those laid down by the UN General Assembly in November 1947 – which would mean for Israel the loss of its part of Jerusalem and a third of the territory it had gained in the fighting. There was no way that Israel would reliquish the New City of Jerusalem, and it needed as much territory as it could hang on to to house its immigrants. Between 1946 and 1947, about 66,000 had come in. In 1948, the number was 101,000; but in 1949 it rose to an all-time peak of 239,000.

The conference dragged on for five months, during which time the UN mediator and his staff were unable to persuade the Arabs and the Israelis to meet officially, though the Israelis did make some secret progress with King Abdullah. One stumbling block was the Arab refugee problem. To help overcome this the Israelis offered to repatriate 100,000 refugees who had been separated from their families. In addition to this they were quite prepared to compensate the families for the land that they had been forced to abandon. The response was disappointing but not surprising. For the Arabs, as always, nothing short of Israel's return of all the land previously held by Arabs was acceptable. The Arabs perceived, too, that the armistice agreements might transform themselves into permanent peace treaties, if they did not stand up for their demands now: permanent peace treaties would also mean formal recognition of Israel's right to exist – something which Arab leaders were not yet ready to concede.

But although talks in Lausanne were moving slowly, in New York the UN made a decision: as country after country declared its support, a resolution by the UN to recognise Israel formally and invite it to become a member was passed on 11 May.

Looking back over the years of constant fighting for recognition, this was an amazing achievement. However, there was little time to sit back and rest on one's laurels. Much work remained to be done in the homeland. One of the Bernadotte proposals which had been thrown out was for limits on immigration to be imposed again; now further thousands of newcomers were making their way to Israel, and they would have to be fed, housed and employed. The new member of the United Nations was on the threshold of great new challenges.

Jews from the Arab states began to come to Israel. One year after the Proclamation of Independence, the brothers of Rina Agagin decided to leave Iraq and try to make it to Israel. Many Jews were successfully bribing Arabs to smuggle them across the intervening borders in lorries:

One day my brothers decided we would go. They met a travel organiser whom we could trust, who was ready to arrange for our departure in exchange for a large amount of money. We knew that since Mother had a vocation and we could go to a kibbutz, everything was going to be just fine; but Mother's family objected that without a husband the work would be too hard for her.

We kids could do nothing, and a year later my mother, who suffered from high blood pressure, died of a stroke. She was only forty-five. In the meantime the Zionist Movement had made a deal with the Prime Minister of Iraq that all Jews could leave and go to Israel. In return, they had to give up their Iraqi citizenship, hand back their passports and ID cards, and sign a document to the effect that they were leaving of their own free will.

Those Jews wishing to leave were given the opportunity to sell their homes and all their household belongings. The sensible ones (as we later learned) made sure that the money which they got was smuggled out of the country. They could travel by any means available – even aeroplanes were put at our disposal. Some left the country secretly, having made undercover arrangements with the Israeli Government. We were not thinking of taking that course. We had a guardian, my mother's uncle, who took care of everything.

I remember the moment when we gathered in the living room and my oldest brother, who was about twenty, together with my second brother, told us about the decision. Then we started to discuss our property and capital. My oldest brother said that we should sell all of it, transfer the money to our family in the USA, and later get it into Israel.

We started to pursue our plan after we had received our guardian's permission. We told him that we wanted to live in a free country without fear and stress. We had an aunt in Israel, but she had stopped writing to us because if you got a letter from Israel at that time you were liable to arrest. There was a lot of anti-Israeli feeling. The Muslim Iraqis organised demonstrations with banners: "Palestine is ours! We will not give it to the Jews!" That scared us. That is why we wanted to go.

My second brother, who was close to twenty, decided to stay and not surrender his passport, so that we could transfer all our capital and properties to his name. We had land, houses and shops. Our neighbours were all selling their household valuables – Persian carpets, gold – and their houses.

We had also inherited a lot of gold from our mother. My older brother sold it – almost 1 kg – and deposited the money in the bank, planning to transfer it to us when we arrived in Israel. We also sold two parcels of land and two shops through an Arab agent who got a good deal for us. In the meantime a friend of my older brother advised him to get his name on to the departure list. "But don't worry," said the friend. "You'll have plenty of time to sell everything and transfer the money." I remember that I had $32,000 and my brother $37,000. We still believed that we had time, and we had people ready and waiting to buy our assets.

Then there was a special announcement on the radio: the government was going to freeze all bank accounts held by Jews, and was going to confiscate all their property. My brother burst into tears, blaming himself for what had happened to our money. We tried to comfort him, because he was a very sensitive and fragile man, and a neighbour of ours had had a fatal heart-attack when he heard the news. We told my brother that the most important thing was to be alive – they would take care of us in Israel.

The next day my two brothers opened our shops and tried to sell what they could. After two days the authorities closed them down: they closed the gold-dealers first. My brothers were very angry and worried about the future. My sister and I went to visit some people who were close to our relatives in the USA and begged them to transfer our money to our family there. They agreed to that, but wouldn't take our gold jewellery. At least there would be something we could call on in Israel when we arrived.

After six weeks we learnt that our turn had come to leave. In the meantime we had had to sell everything we owned for very little money in order to buy food. We once had beautiful furniture and rare Persian carpets. Towards the end we were forced to break up furniture and use it to make a fire to heat bathwater: but equally we didn't want to leave it behind for the Arabs to enjoy.

The day of our departure came and my sister and I joined the others in the courtyard of the synagogue with our bags. My oldest brother had already left for Israel. We were each allowed 20 kg of personal belongings. I took clothes and a light blanket. It was very hard to decide what to leave behind.

The airport was not too far away and we were taken there by taxi. Before we boarded, they weighed our bags and if they weighed more than 20 kg we had to take things out.

I was very sad because I was worried about the brother who was left behind having to pay back all the deposit money that we'd had from various would-be purchasers. I was sad too because I was leaving the country I was born and raised in, with no hope of ever seeing it again, even for a visit.

At the airport they separated the men from the women and checked us very thoroughly to see if we were carrying anything illegal. In one room they opened our bags and turned everything out on to the floor. I had my parents' photographs, and souvenirs from my childhood and school, but when I tried to collect them one of the Iraqi guards pushed me away and said that they would put everything back, which, of course, they didn't. We found out later that they were stealing things for themselves.

We were put in a huge tent to wait for the aeroplane. Soon afterwards, there was an announcement: the plane was defective and we would have to wait for another few hours. We waited from 10 p.m. until 3 a.m. The Zionists provided us with sandwiches, and an Iraqi policemen kept guard over us. They took all the women's handbags and threw them into a big pile, promising that we would get them back when we boarded.

I begged to be allowed to keep mine, and finally they agreed to let me.

By the time we boarded we were very tired. We arrived in Tel Aviv at 6 a.m. As we were landing, I looked out of the small windows for my first sight of Israel. When we got out of the plane many kneeled and kissed the ground. I did not. I looked around and through the fence I could see people going to work, leading a normal life. There was joy and happiness in the air.

Very soon after landing I had my first disappointment. They gave us tea in cardboard cups and simple dark bread of a kind I'd never tasted before, spread with marmalade. Then they gave us temporary papers and took us to a centre where they sprayed newcomers from the Arab states with DDT. We were told to bend down and lift our hair for the spraying, but I wouldn't. Somehow I managed to get away from that humiliating process, and I also avoided the TB immunisation.

Then we had to wait until we were taken by lorry to the railway station. My suitcase hadn't arrived, but they told me I would be able to pick it up later at Sha'ah Aliyah, which means literally "the gate of the immigration to Israel". Luckily I had some personal items in my handbag.

The next disappointment was the train. It was made up of cattle trucks, and the trip to Hadera lasted six hours, because the train stopped so frequently. It was dark by the time we arrived. They gave us camp beds and told us we would have to sleep under the sky.

The next day we were taken to Sha'ah Aliyah. There we saw bungalows, each with a few beds in them. They gave us food coupons. There was a communal dining-room, but those with families could eat separately if they so wished.

There were newcomers from all over the place, including Romania, but we couldn't find anyone from our home town. However, I could speak French, so I could communicate with the Romanians.

The toilets were filthy.

My oldest brother was already living in Qiryat Ono. He'd told us to ask to be transferred there too, but they wanted to send us somewhere else. I refused, and told them that we were orphans and that we wanted to be together; in the end it was arranged. When we left, they gave us enough money to cover our food for the first few days. When we arrived at Qiryat Ono we found that our tent was a long way from the gate and as we walked towards it carrying our heavy suitcases we sank into the soft sand. It was horrible – a nightmare!

We were each given a bed, some thin blankets, a loaf and a few cans of food. At night we saw all kinds of creeping creatures on the thick material the tent was made of. I will not forget that first night as long as I live. I was really very devastated and upset. This was not what I had dreamt about. But I knew that we had no choice.

My other brother arrived safely, but our brothers didn't want us to work, since in Iraq girls normally never worked. Our brothers went to work in the construction industry, doing digging and any hard labour they could get from the employment agency.

Leah Rachmani was pregnant with her third child when she arrived in Tehran to get the documents she needed to go to Israel to join her parents:

Then I travelled by bus to Turkey, and from there boarded a ship which took us to Israel. I had sold nearly everything and all the belongings I had left were wet and torn when we arrived. On the ship, we slept in bunks. My younger son was crying but the man in charge helped us. The bread we had was the best I'd ever tasted.

We had problems when we arrived. Our friends who came to meet us said, "Why did you come?" That scared us instead of encouraging us. But they were concerned for my husband, who was a merchant back home, and they were worried that he might not be able to join me for some time.

We were taken to Sha'ah Aliyah – a transit camp for new immigrants. There they gave us a wooden cabin, beds and blankets, and three meals a day. We even had running water, and the food was cooked for us so we didn't have to bother with anything. Each cabin was huge and every family got a space in it with one bed for everyone. But there were no partitions, and no privacy. There were about ten families in each cabin. My sons were five and three years old and I was pregnant with my son Saul. We stayed there a whole month. Then, through my father's connections, we got a "better" place at Ain Hanasi. There we shared a tent with one other family. The beds were made of a wooden board on four iron legs. The mattress was filled with straw. There were no cooking facilities and everything in general was tough.

We did get food coupons which enabled us to prepare some meals from what was in the packages we got; but to get these coupons we had to queue from six in the morning. Sometimes when we got to the head of the queue they had run out and we came home crying. There was a standard package for everyone. Children were entitled to two eggs per week; adults could have only one. A pregnant woman was allowed one chicken a month, that's all. I used to keep my chicken alive so that I could get more eggs for the children. Milk, though, we did have.

Beef was a problem. We got 1 lb per family per month. The meat was not fresh and very hard to eat. Fruit and vegetables you could also only get with coupons – you even had to have a coupon for an onion. Later, they brought nurses to teach us how to take care of the children, and they started the immunisation programme, which is one of the best in the world now. They also taught us how to make porridge for the babies.

My older son was accepted for school, but there was still no kindergarten in those days for the younger one. I gave birth to Saul in the cabin. They told me that there were male doctors in the hospitals, and in our culture we were not used to being touched by strange men. Luckily my great aunt was in the same camp and she came to help me.

My husband joined me, and soon after that I was pregnant again. In the meantime, though, we had moved to a block of flats built of stone in Bet She'an, in the Jordan valley, near the Jordanian border. This was already a great luxury. Almost as soon as we were in our new flat I went into labour and I had no help. I was alone with my one-year-old baby.

I went out and gathered some sand from the building site nearby, and I sat on the mound I had made and had my baby. My husband had gone off to seek help. He found a young woman who was able to come and watch over the newborn baby while I rested. I slept for two hours and then I got up and fixed my one-year-old his porridge on our Primus stove.

My husband worked wherever he could, in the fields, planting trees, and in the neighbouring kibbutzim. Today people are spoilt. They sit and wait for jobs to come to them and they are very choosy and picky. I did not work outside the flat because I had to take care of my children. In the end I had eleven children, so I had my hands full! Back in Iran my husband had a shop; he sold all kinds of fabrics, wool, silk and cotton and so on. He was a very intelligent man – he could turn his hand to anything; but he wanted to work and make money fast. He worked very hard, and my life was very tough too because I did not have the luxury women have today. I worked at home from sunrise until late at night to give my children everything I could.

I am happy and proud to say that all my children went on to higher education, and they are very successful in their lives. But I would like to tell you that I got married at the age of thirteen. I did not know my husband until the wedding night – unlike young people today who spend years together before they get married. My parents agreed the marriage with my husband's parents and we had no say. I had my third child before I was twenty years old.

Eli Amir was twelve, and the eldest son, when he arrived in Israel from Iraq, part of a family of nine:

We came here by plane straight from Baghdad Airport to Lydda. All nine of us in one aircraft. It was the first time we had ever flown. We were about to enter the Promised Land. A dream of 2,500 years was about to come true. We came dressed in our best clothes, and the mood on the aeroplane was so happy! People were singing and dancing in the aisle. It was really something.

Before we left Baghdad I asked my father to describe Israel. He said, "Imagine that you were in a beautiful garden and that you were looking at the beautiful flowers." Baghdad is a beautiful city and early on *Shabat* you can smell the beautiful smell of the flowers in the morning. My father said, "The country of Israel looks like the colour purple, a royal purple with a great smell, a lovely smell."

That was how he described the country. At the time I said to myself, God, can you tell me why my father sounds like a madman, describing a country that looks purple and smells good? Even Paradise isn't as good as what he's talking about. So, we arrived in Israel and what did we find? We found tents, we found mud, and we found sand.

We were taken to a camp near Haifa with thousands of people living in tents surrounded by a wire fence to make sure you couldn't get out. It was like the Tower of Babel – we saw people such as we had never seen and heard languages we had never heard:

there were Romanians, Poles, Moroccans and Libyans – to name but a few.

So this was the purple and scented land? The shock we felt that day as we walked through the camp in our suits and ties remains with me even now. You must understand that we were very much influenced by the British way of life. Our second language was English; we wore English clothes; the intelligentsia imitated the British by drinking tea with milk. So, we walked through this camp in our English suits and ties, even with trilbys like Humphrey Bogart wore in *Casablanca*. And there were the tents. Our dream was broken.

But there were some pleasant surprises too. In Baghdad we didn't have many blond people. I was twelve and a half and I was a very sensitive boy. I remember there was a blonde girl in the camp, dressed in shorts. When I saw her I was shocked. Such dress for a woman in Baghdad would have been unheard of.

Most Muslim women at that time covered their faces and their bodies. They were entirely swathed in black. When I saw this girl in shorts, I covered my face with my hands. But I was curious. I opened my fingers and saw a woman's legs for the first time in my life. My God! After two minutes I found that I was the only man daft enough to be so self-conscious about looking at her!

But despite this pleasure I felt that God had betrayed me. We had come to a country where we didn't speak the language. There were new smells, like the smell of the sea. Iraq has no sea. And there were mountains – they were new, too, because Baghdad is flat. There are mountains only in the north of Iraq. So, the landscape was different, the language was different, the people were different, the food was different and on top of all that there we were sharing a tent with ten strangers!

My family lived in such conditions for seven years. My Dad couldn't find a job; and not only him, but thousands of others. The government gave us three primitive and simple meals a day. For a year or so we used to go around stealing potatoes, aubergines, cucumbers, anything we could get. I was lucky. After a year I was sent to a kibbutz.

The influx of settlers continued, and by October 1950 it all but exceeded the country's ability to absorb them. Although the generosity of Jews overseas had guaranteed that money was available, keeping pace with the building programme was difficult. Only one-third of the planned accommodation had been completed. A harsh winter had forced a diversion of funds, to be used for the purchase of corrugated-iron huts which, although bearable in winter, were extremely hot during Israel's long summers. But desperate times call for desperate measures, and the waves of new immigrants had to be housed, come what may.

When corrugated metal for the sides of the huts ran out, canvas was shipped in and nailed to wooden frames. Thousands of these shelters became temporary homes for many of those who arrived in the country during this period; and, amazing as it may seem, not one of the thousands who arrived in Israel during this period was ever forced to sleep outdoors.

But the most important thing of all was that the homeland was there. Sheltering and permanent. As the prophet Isaiah had written, "They shall build houses, and inhabit them; and they shall plant vineyards, and eat the fruit of them. They shall not build, and another inhabit; they shall not plant, and another eat: for as the days of a tree are the days of my people, and mine elect shall long enjoy the work of their hands."

Bibliography

David Ben-Gurion, ed. *The Jews in their Land*
Larry Collins and Dominique LaPierre *O Jerusalem*
Uri Dan *To the Promised Land*
Ben Dunkelman *Dual Allegiance: An Autobiography*
Abba Eban *Heritage – Civilisation and the Jews*
Martin Gilbert *Jerusalem*
Anton Gill *The Journey back from Hell*
Hermann Kinder and Werner Hilgemann, eds. *dtv-Atlas Zur Weltgeschichte*
    Vol. 2
Dan Kurzman *Ben-Gurion, Prophet of Fire*
Walter Laqueur and Barry Rubin, eds. *The Arab/Israel Reader*
Golda Meir *My Life*
Conor Cruise O'Brien *The Siege*
Ritchie Ovendale *The Middle East since 1914*
Shimon Peres *Battling for Peace: Memoirs*
Gertrude Samuels *B.G. Fighter of Goliaths. The story of Ben-Gurion*
Yitzhak Shamir *Summing Up: An Autobiography*
Leonard Slater *The Pledge*